ALCOHOL RECOVERY

How To Control and Stop Drinking Excess Alcohol

(An Easy Guide to Stop Drinking and Recover From Alcohol Addiction)

Tiana Wygant

Published By Simon Dough

Tiana Wygant

All Rights Reserved

Alcohol Recovery: How To Control and Stop Drinking Excess Alcohol (An Easy Guide to Stop Drinking and Recover From Alcohol Addiction)

ISBN 978-1-77485-346-7

All rights reserved. No part of this guide may be reproduced in any form without permission in writing from the publisher except in the case of brief quotations embodied in critical articles or reviews.

Legal & Disclaimer

The information contained in this book is not designed to replace or take the place of any form of medicine or professional medical advice. The information in this book has been provided for educational and entertainment purposes only.

The information contained in this book has been compiled from sources deemed reliable, and it is accurate to the best of the Author's knowledge; however, the Author cannot guarantee its accuracy and validity and cannot be held liable for any errors or omissions. Changes are periodically made to this book. You must consult your doctor or get professional medical advice before using any of the suggested remedies, techniques, or information in this book.

Upon using the information contained in this book, you agree to hold harmless the Author from and against any damages, costs, and expenses, including any legal fees potentially resulting from the application of any of the information provided by this guide. This disclaimer applies to any damages or injury caused by the use and application, whether directly or indirectly, of any advice or information presented, whether for breach of contract, tort, negligence, personal injury, criminal intent, or under any other cause of action.

You agree to accept all risks of using the information presented inside this book. You need to consult a professional medical practitioner in order to ensure you are both able and healthy enough to participate in this program.

TABLE OF CONTENTS

INTRODUCTION 1

CHAPTER 1: WHAT IS THE FIRST STEP TO QUITTING? 4

CHAPTER 2: ADMISSION, HOPE, SURRENDER 12

CHAPTER 3: MAINTAINING YOUR NEWFOUND SOBRIETY IN THE LONG IN THE LONG TERM 24

CHAPTER 4: WHAT IS DRUG CLASSIFICATION? 31

CHAPTER 5: THE REASONS PEOPLE ARE ADDICTED TO ALCOHOL 60

CHAPTER 6: WHY SHOULD YOU UNDERGO WITHDRAWAL AND TREATMENT FOR ALCOHOL ADDICTION? 63

CHAPTER 7: UNDERSTANDING ALCOHOLISM 66

CHAPTER 8: STARTING THE SOBER JOURNEY SAFELY 73

CHAPTER 9: TIPS AND TRICKS TO SUCCESSFULLY STOP DRINKING ALCOHOL TIPS AND RECOMMENDATIONS 77

CHAPTER 10: COMMITTING TO CHANGE 93

CHAPTER 11: ALTER THE WAY YOU DRINK 96

CHAPTER 12: ONLINE SUPPORT GROUP 101

CHAPTER 13: WHAT IS DRUG CLASSIFICATION? 104

CHAPTER 14: CREATE GOALS AND BE KIND TO YOURSELF 125

CHAPTER 15: THE STEPS TO GET RID OF ALCOHOL 132

CHAPTER 16: NEGATIVE SIDE EFFECTS OF DRINKING UNDERAGE 139

CHAPTER 17: ACTIONS TO RECOVERY AND AVOIDING RELAPSES 159

CHAPTER 18: DISAPPEARING TIME TRICK 163

CHAPTER 19: REMAIN SOBER AND TAKE ADVANTAGE OF THE REWARDS 178

CONCLUSION 184

Introduction

This is the ultimate step-by-step guide that provides you with all the necessary assistance you require to get your decision about quitting alcoholism a reality. It is common for people to have the notion about quitting drink as impossible.

It's not true! In reality, the road is rough and lengthy, which requires determination to fight off the temptations that may come on the way. If you're looking to stop drinking, you'll discover all the information you need in this article to get your goal a reality.

The book contains methods that have been tested by people who have succeeded in using the methods and health officials who have made guidelines. Recovering from alcohol dependence and alcoholism is easy when you've decided to do it. This is regardless of the kind of addiction or strength you possess.

This guide will ensure that you never have to wait to the point that you're "bankrupt" or do not have enough money to allow it to function. The purpose of this guide is to be available at anytime, as long as you've made your decision.

The steps are simple and easy to follow, makes them easy to follow and adapt to your way of life. It dispels the false of alcoholism by making the process easy and simple. Additionally, you'll learn the path to take for your own life, such as where and how to access help and treatment should it need to be.

"Self Guide to Overcoming Alcoholism" was made to make sure that you don't require any willpower, nor feel any deprivation or self-deprivation throughout the process. All your anxieties will be removed, allowing it possible to enjoy the most on all occasions.

It is important to be aware of that when you take the decision to stop drinking completely, you are giving yourself an opportunity to start anew life! This is the time to begin making plans and goals for your life and follow them with a great degree of success. You'll be surprised by how great your life is going to be.

I am certain that while writing this book, there will be thousands of people who would like to stop drinking the majority of them teens who are addicted. Most people view alcoholism as an option due to the bitterness that they experience in their lives, maybe following the breakup of a relationship or the loss of someone they cherish. Many people lose their jobs or lose their job and opt for alcohol to forget about this! Alcohol does not cause one to forget anything, but it provides a false impression of the reality. Numerous have succeeded and I'm sure you'll be able to do the same!

Chapter 1: What is the First Step to Quitting?

We all wish to make our lives better in some way. If you're reading this article, then you are probably thinking of taking a major change to your the way you live, and making the crucial decision to stop drinking alcohol completely. Sometimes, things are out of hand and before you're able to notice it, it gets out of control. It can be difficult to determine the best way to eliminate the alcohol addiction from your routine or daily habits once you've been suffering from addiction for the longest time. With this helpful guide, you'll be able to alter your lifestyle and be well on your way towards becoming the person you wish to be. It's likely to be an extended time since you've had contact with your true self However, believe in your ability to become the person you want to be, all you have to do is make sure you take an action every single day and you'll become the person you want to be!

The first step in getting rid of your addiction to alcohol drinks is to enter the right mind-set in your mind. You've begun your journey by deciding you'd like to quit and then figuring out the best method to achieve it. When you've made that important decision to end your addiction it is best to remind yourself why you're making the decision. It's crucial to understand there are many different levels of dependence that you need to consider. Around seventeen million Americans are believed to suffer from an alcohol dependence disorder (AUD) which means in truth, you're not the only one in your battle. The figures also cover alcoholism, as well as dangerous drinking behaviors that do not attain the degree of dependence, however. It is possible that you haven't considered yourself an alcohol user however this doesn't mean that you shouldn't require assistance to overcome the habit you're stuck in. Everyone could benefit from some positive advice every now and then particularly when we are struggling with a severe addiction.

You might be thinking about what you should do once you've taken this major decision that is going to alter your life for ever. The most straightforward things to consider is the main reason you're no longer going to consume alcohol. Spend some time and create an outline of the many things alcohol does to you and all the things you do not enjoy about it. The list you make is very personal therefore, yours will not be the same as anyone else's. However there are some ideas to consider:

Money

Alcohol consumption can be an expensive activity, particularly when you are in an establishment or bar. Even if you're drinking in your home at night, the price isn't one to overlook and can mount up quite quickly over the course of the course of. It is still expensive to drink when you buy massive quantities of it or purchasing it on a regular basis. Consider what you could do using all that money. You could put aside money to go on a trip and put the money towards the tuition fund for your child or pay off the mortgage, make investments in stock, purchase a brand new automobile, and the list goes on.

Health

A little bit of alcohol isn't terribly unhealthy for your health however, if you're drinking regularly enough to make it an issue in your daily life, then you're definitely impacting your health negatively. Every year , around 85,000 people die due to alcohol-related illnesses throughout the United States alone and that amount is growing. The majority of those deaths stem due to diseases of the kidney, liver and other vital organs essential for the health of humans. In addition, excessive use can make you gain excess weight. It is easy to consume calories in the absence of you drink and are most likely to choose bad decisions regarding food when being drunk. In my case, when I was a alcoholic, I had gained over 50 pounds. The primary reason was that, during my drinking spell which I prefer to refer to it, I'd indulge in whatever I desired. I still recall those times when I would gobble down a huge cheese pizza in front of my face. This can really take the strain on your body for a long time!

Relationships

It's difficult to hold your tongue while drinking, which is why you may begin engaging in heated debates with your loved ones more often being under the influence of alcohol. This can make it harder for you to stick to your promises of appointments, or even to take a moment to consider if you're harming the feelings of someone else. Take a moment to consider it, and record the negative ways in which your behavior is impacting your relationships.

Career

It is possible that you will do the same job as you always have making sure you are on time and doing your job. Do you ever arrive at work after a night of drinking? Do you occasionally call in because of alcohol consumption? Perhaps you don't really care about work and are waiting until the bell rings and you are able to get out and have some drinks. It's possible that your drinking habits aren't considered to be serious, but consider all the ways your lifestyle is hindering your work, and the opportunities that it's taking from you.

If you're aware of any other areas where alcohol influences negatively in your life , be sure to write them down also. After spending some time with this list, these problems will be pleasant to be fresh and clear in your thoughts. The next step is to remember! The list should be placed up on the walls, on your refrigerator, or the bathroom mirror. It is important to keep these negative consequences in a prominent location in a place where you will be able to see them and look them up whenever you're attracted to grab an alcoholic beverage and you will be eventually enticed and at the least, initially.

Chapter 2: Admission, Hope, Surrender

The admission of powerlessness

Accept that you are in no position to conquer addiction and that your life has become overwhelming.

A lot of addicts begin their addiction because of curiosity, when they're teenagers or children, while some are hooked due to an unjustifiable need for prescription drugs. A lot of people begin their addiction before they're even teenagers while others aren't aware of the issue until they're in their late 20s when they're college-aged. Whatever it was which brought you here; you decided to take it due to the substance you took to fill an empty space that was more than the pain.

Very rarely, those affected by their addictions admit to being addicted. To conceal the seriousness of their situation and to keep from being discovered and suffering their consequences, they try to hide their actions. They were later informed of the truth by a family member or a judge, doctor or even a religious leader in the past before they were unable to conceal the truth. The addiction is ruining their lives. It's destroying your life.

The first step in recovery from addiction is acknowledging that you're in power with regards to the addiction that you suffer from, and that the situation has become overwhelming.

When you're ready to do this, you'll be able to complete certain of the next action steps.

Abstain from drinking.

Every person's addiction is unique However, some facts don't differ. There is no way to begin without the determination to start it. The journey to freedom from addiction and uncleanliness begins with a flickering of determination.

It is said that when the suffering of addiction gets more than the discomfort of the solution, they'll choose to stay away from the habit. Are you at this point? Are you prepared to abstain?

If you're still not to the point where you are feeling that you do not want to give up from drinking, then you could try the following exercise.

Recognize that you're not ready to not abstain.

Get a piece and a pencil and record what your addiction costs you.

Examine if you're willing let those costs go on.

An example of what your alcohol addiction could cost you can be found in the following.

There's something wrong with those relationships that you are currently in, be it with coworkers, friends family members, relatives, or even your spouse.

You are depressed, embarrassed and anxious constantly.

Drinking is hindering your family obligations and job performance.

Your health is in decline.

You've been laid off from your job or profession due to drinking.

Be humble and let go of Pride

Honesty and pride aren't two of the same. They can't be in the same space. The illusion of pride is the basis of addiction. Pride will distort your reality and alter the facts in the present and have been and will become. This is a barrier in your journey to recovery.

If you're willing to refrain from speaking out and admitting the problem that you are confronted with, your pride will be replaced by humility.

Admit Your Problem, Find Help, Attend Meetings

When you engage in your addiction you are lying to yourself and to other people. However, you aren't able to fool yourself. You may appear to be in a good mood filled with excuses and bravado, yet in your heart you know. You're aware that you're sliding down an insidious slope that's sure to bring more pain. It's hard work, but it's also a relief to acknowledge you're suffering. There's a tiny window for hope to be able to see in your daily life.

If you can, go to recovery meetings whenever you can in order to be hopeful. You must attend these meetings in order to meet people who have been through the same struggles like you. They can be your guides and assist you on the slippery road to recovery. You'll only find faith as well as understanding and help in meetings for recovery; not judgement and hatred, nor anger.

Believe in Hope

We believed that an entity greater than ourselves could bring us back to normal.

Although you don't need to be religious in order to take part in the AA program or recovery from addiction however, you should be aware of the strength out there that is spiritual, or the members of the AA club you're part of which can assist you through your journey to recovery. Be confident and believe that other people will be with you during the process. They will assist you in learning how to conquer the difficult steps towards becoming completely clean.

The addicts who are addicted to alcohol and other substances are discouraged that they will ever recover, that they'll be able to lead normal lives, and they'll be able speak to their family and friends again , without the shadow of addiction hovering over them. They give up on living a life of normality and happiness which doesn't require them to have that last drink before bed, or the first sip when they get up early in the day. The addiction to alcohol is a real and dangerous addiction that takes over your whole existence, but it is possible to fight it.

Even though you're not able to control your addiction, you're not in a position to make choices about your life.

Participate in Meetings

Even if these meetings are not religious, if they have a religious inclination attend these meetings and get engulfed by the warmth of others. Enjoy the warmth of their compassion. They will not make assumptions about you, regardless of whether they believe faith in God or not. They're here to assist you in understanding what's going on and how you can be hopeful that you can have more positive, brighter future.

Read Recovery Stories

If you're unable join in with meetings at first because of your personal beliefs, or you're scared to show your personal story to other people who have been through similar experiences, you might be interested in reading several recovery stories on the internet. Find stories that truly inspire you. There are many who been through the same thing as you today, and they're ready to discuss their successes as well as their mistakes to you, so you understand the lessons you need to be looking towards in the future.

Make Sure You Take Care of Yourself

Be prepared for mood swings and combat your cravings by eating well and getting enough sleep. Exercise can also release endorphins that ease your stressand boost your wellbeing. All of these will allow you to feel hopeful in your work.

Develop your Support Network

Find positive people and influencers that inspire you to feel positive about yourself. If you are more involved with the lives of others and your community by joining an AA chapter and AA, you'll have of things to gain. This helps you stay focused.

Find new interests and activities to pursue.

Find new activities, hobbies or work that makes you feel like you are a valuable person with some purpose to live by. When you accomplish this, you'll feel more fulfilled and drinking won't have as much of an appeal for you.

Continue Treatment

Don't stop taking care of yourself because you've had a bad day or you make a mistake. Always attend your meetings with AA to renew your faith every day. It is the hope that keeps you clean for the rest in your existence.

Surrender

Give your wishes and life to someone else's care.

This is the first step to take. You've acknowledged that you're struggling and you're hopeful that you'll be able to get over it, but you must surrender to the wisdom and knowledge of someone else. This is perhaps the most significant move you'll ever make. It's the time to surrender control of your life, and allow others in the group as well as your sponsor to guide you towards the path of sobriety and independence.

When you reach this stage you'll realize that you have made the decision to make your own choices. You recognize that the decision to change your life to this point is your choice and not the decision of anyone else. You know that your spouse, parents as well as your children aren't capable of making this decision for you.

Participate in Religious Services

It doesn't matter which religion you'd like to follow it is important to attend a few events even if it's not your primary reason to adhere to God at this time. These events will increase your belief that you're following the proper path. You can also join a group of people who are atheists within your region.

Change What You Can , and Accept What You Don't

This is an important moment for you. There are some things that can alter in the present and the into the future, but you need to recognize that what you did in the past was unchangeable. When you're able to get past it then you are able to proceed to the next stage.

This can be done by recognizing that the past has been set in stone while the future isn't. Take whatever steps you need to recognize that you are not able change the past, but you are able to alter the future. There is hope, and there is a bright spot towards the light at the end tunnel.

Rely on Friends and Family

Being surrounded by those you cherish and who support you will make it easier to feel secure when you give in to the fact that you are an alcohol addict. They will aid you when you are feeling an urge to drink or feel weak.

Create an Sober Social Network

You can not only go to AA meetings however, you also can meet people in the same position as you, and have a blast in social gatherings with them. Find establishments that don't serve alcohol, so you can go out for a night of fun without alcohol. Find people who are supportive of your decision to stay sober.

Plan your meetings to be a priority

If you are a part of a recovery organization and regularly attend weekly meetings you will be able to feel more relaxed. They know what you're experiencing So let them assist you!

Chapter 3: Maintaining Your Newfound Sobriety In The Long In The Long Term

As you may have read in the last chapter, breaking the cycle of addiction to alcohol isn't an easy task; the process requires commitment and sacrifice. Not just from your side but also from the side of your friends and family members. Additionally, it is likely to trigger some withdrawal symptoms. It is not wise to allow yourself to slip into a relapse.

However, the odds of relapses are significant and very real. It is because addiction to alcohol as with any other type of addiction, isn't something which is "cured" however it is something you have to overcome by committing yourself on an regular basis. Be aware that it takes dedication determination, discipline, and the courage to keep going with the positive changes that you need to achieve.

Long-term sobriety is a task that requires a lot of effort from you. Also, you have to be mindful and aware of your choices particularly ones that have to involve alcohol. The key is the ability to recognize the triggers that lead to alcohol and develop effective strategies to combat the triggers, and also to set an appropriate support system around you to help keep your commitments to your goals.

A few of the most important actions you can take to ensure you live a clean lifestyle are listed below.

1. Stay healthy

A healthy lifestyle can make you feel physically as well as mentally healthier and help you in dealing with triggers in your day-to-day life (like stress) which are good for your health. Start by being particular about your diet choices. Also, live an active life. Go to the gym or do regular workout routines at your home. Make time for rest and relaxation to take the burden off your shoulders. Research has proven how when your body's in good condition, you not only build up stamina but you also have a more positive self-esteem. That's because when look and feel great, you be more satisfied of the person you are. When you're satisfied with yourself it is likely that you won't need alcohol to make up for it.

2. Do the things you love

Also, follow your passions through the things you enjoy doing. If you're occupied with things you're happy to do, you have no reason for you to reach for bottles to deal with your triggers. If you don't have any interests or hobbies that are healthy, take a look at different activities and select those you like the most. This might include engaging in a physical or educational class as well as joining a team, learning a new craft or other activity that you like and doesn't include drinking!

3. Make sure you surround yourself with the right People

A lot of us drink or continue to drink due to the company we have drinks. If a lot of your family and friends are drinkers, it is advised to form a group of acquaintances who are clean as well as spend some time with them. A network of friends who are clean can assist you in keeping sober. It doesn't mean that you have to shut off your family members and friends who drink in any way However, at first it's best to avoid engaging with drinkers when you're not drinking (i.e. not in the bar). When you get to a point when you're better equipped to manage your behaviour, it's easier to be able to interact with these friends regardless of whether or not they are drinking alcohol. At first the presence of a strong network of friends who don't drink can assist in keeping you from drinking.

Your family and friends are also crucial in helping you get over your addiction. It is vital for them to be aware of your goals and be supportive of your efforts to achieve them. Most of the time, it's these family members who are most affected by your alcoholism and therefore will have the greatest benefit. Therefore, they are likely to help you. Be sure to rely on them when facing difficult times during your recovery.

In the previous chapter Support organizations (like Alcoholics Anonymous) can also be a fantastic source of people who will help you in keeping your sobriety.

4. Learn from any previous attempts at sobriety

The problem with the process of becoming sober is that a lot of people are prone to relapse, and often several times. If you've tried to get sober before but failed, it is a good idea to think about the things that worked and did not work, and how you'll incorporate these experiences into your plan to become more sober in the future. If you are on a attempt to get sober again, it's advantageous to record what is working and what's not. Utilize these lessons regularly to improve and adjust your treatment plans.

5. Use A Journal

Write in a journal down your thoughts and experiences regarding your healing. The act of writing down your thoughts isn't just an outlet for remembrance and healing, but it's also a great way to deal with your current situation. If you've set weekly, daily, or monthly goals for your drinking habits A journal could be a place where you note down your progress and keep track of what you're doing.

6. Review Your Goals

If you are tempted to drink, think about it for a while and reflect on the goals you set at the start of your path to sobriety. In the end you'll likely had a good grasp of many, but not all of those objectives. Be aware of how important these goals are to you , and the risk of drinking that could jeopardize the achievement of those goals. If the goals you originally sketched out don't seem to be relevant anymore Then make the effort to set new goals. This is crucial because it gives you motivation to become and remaining sober.

Chapter 4: What is Drug Classification?

Drug classifications help categorize substances into categories.

The classification of drugs based on similarities to substances is crucial because chemically similar drugs typically have the same effects and risk. A person who is dependent on a drug is more likely to abuse it, and may rely on a different drug which is chemically related. In spite of these generalities, chemically similar drugs can be different in terms of legal and medical consequences.

A lot of people categorize substances based on their effects on the body and mind For instance, certain substances can make one feel vigorous and energetic, while others produce more tranquility.

The majority of countries have a legal class system of drugs. They determine the conditions in which the drug is legally legal and the various regulations for the drug, as well as any fines imposed by law relating to distribution, ownership or manufacturing. Legal classifications often are determined by the therapeutic value of the medication and the recognized dangers.

There is a debate about the way that drugs should be classified in the eyes of experts. This means that the same medication can be classified in two different groups with identical names. Because of these differences there is no way to establish the "definitive" group of classifications for drugs.

Drug Classifications Based On Chemical Makeup

Alcohol

Alcohol is the most frequently abused substance in the world and this includes the U.S. Alcohols affect a variety of organ systems and poses a number of dangers for users. Consuming alcohol triggers feelings of euphoria, and reduces inhibitions. Additionally, it can cause visual impairment. Alcohol is a central nervous system depressant. They cause the most regrettable and long-term harm on the liver. There are numerous types of alcohol consumption that include:

Beer.

Wine.

Liquor.

Opioids

Opioids, also known as opiates can be made by opium, a drug, or are substances that are designed to mimic the effects of it. Opioids function by interfering with the heart's neurotransmitters and block the messages they send. They can serve as powerful painkillers however, they can also cause extreme pleasure and lead to dependence. Opioid addiction is among the most serious issues faced in America in the present. They are among the most addictive of the chemicals that are known and one of the most fatal. The most well-known opioids are:

Heroin.

Fentanyl.

Oxycodone.

Benzodiazepines

Benzodiazepines or Benzos are a category of drugs that function by interfering with the neurotransmitter gamma-aminobutyric acids (GABA-A). Every Benzo reacts to GABA in a variety of ways, and that is the reason each Benzo impacts the brain and body differently. Benzos are advised to treat various disorders of rest and psychiatry However, they are often misused. Benzos are extremely addictive and can cause a variety of mental and physical difficulties. The types of Benzos include:

Ativan.

Valium.

Xanax.

Cannabinoids

Cannabinoids are a category of substances which are chemically related with tetrahydrocannabinol (THC) which is the active ingredient in marijuana. Cannabinoids produce feelings of happiness However, they negatively impact physical and mental health. Cannabinoids are among the most frequently used and abused drug after alcohol, and are gaining more legal acceptance. While they are considered to be less addictive than other classifications, they can impact a person's mental and physical health. Cannabinoids can be classified into:

Marijuana.

Hashish.

Barbiturates

Barbiturates impede the function that the brain and central nervous system performs. they are the derivatives of the chemical barbituric acidity. Barbiturates were traditionally used for treating sleep disorders and psychiatric disorders as well as anesthesia, and other ailments like headache and epilepsy. Barbiturates are extremely addictive and they carry a high chance of overdose because they can trigger several organs in the body to stop functioning.

Barbiturates are classified into three types:

Amytal.

Luminal.

Pentobarbital.

The classification of Drugs based on Effects

Depressants

They are also known by the name of "downers," depressants create feelings of tiredness and relaxation. Although many have legitimate reasons such as fighting insomnia and mental disorders however, they are often misused because they can induce feelings of happiness. Depressions aren't the only of the most addictive drugs however they're among the most dangerous and are most likely to trigger an overdose. The types of depressants are:

Alcohol.

Opiates.

Barbiturates.

Stimulants

Also called "uppers," the first purpose of stimulants is to boost concentration, energy and alertness. They are believed to trigger an adrenaline high i.e energy. Since a certain time it is believed that stimulants increase efficiency and performance and also induce feelings of pleasure. In time, stimulants become extremely addictive and carry an extremely high chance of misuse. Some types of stimulants include:

Adderall.

Cocaine.

Meth.

Hallucinogens

Hallucinogens, sometimes referred to as dissociative affect the user's perception of reality which can result in visual and auditory hallucinations often referred to by the term "tripping." While hallucinogens can be less dependent than other classifications of drugs but they're typically more severe and risky. Some hallucinogens include:

LSD.

Psilocybin Mushrooms.

PCP.

Inhalants

Inhalants are a vast array of chemical compounds that are ingested mostly by breathing them in or exhaling. Inhalants are mostly used substances that aren't suitable for consumption by humans. There's a broad range of inhalants available, the majority of them induce feelings of increased energy. Inhalants are not as well-studied as other substances; however, while they're generally more addictive than other substances but the use of inhalants is risky and can cause adverse health consequences. Commonly abused inhalants are:

Paint thinner.

Remove polish from your toenails.

Gasoline

The Federal government approved The Controlled Chemicals Do Something Act in 1970 as a response to the rising drug problem. The legislation established five classifications of drugs. What uses a substance is based on the validity and its possible medical applications, coupled with the potential for addiction and addiction. America must categorize the use of particular substances using schedules in order to adhere to agreements with diplomatic institutions, such as those in the Single Convention on Narcotic Drugs.

Schedule V

Drugs in the class of Program V are the least regulated and the lowest penalties of any classification of drugs. The Plan V drugs have the most accepted medical use and have a lower risk of addiction as compared to Timetable IV drugs, and have a lower chance of becoming addicts as compared to Schedule IV drugs. For example:

Lomotil.

Motoren.

Lyrica

Schedule IV

Plan IV drugs have regulations and penalties among Timetable V and Routine III drugs. Plan IV drugs are the most accepted medical use and a very low chance of abuse; and a low risk of cravings. For example:

Ambien.

Darvocet.

Tramadol

Schedule III

Schedule III drugs have higher restrictions and more severe fines as compared to

Regular IV drugs and fewer regulations and less severe penalties in comparison to Plan II drugs. Schedule III drugs offer the most effective medical benefits and a lower risk of abuse than Regimen II and I medications; in addition, they have a lower risk of addiction. Some of the types that belong to Plan III drugs include:

Anabolic steroids.

Ketamine.

Vicodin.

Schedule II

Schedule II drugs come with more rules and higher fines than other drug, excluding the Regular We drugs. Schedule II drugs are the most effective in terms of medical benefits, but they also have a higher risk of abuse and a significant dependence risk. The types that are part of Timetable II drugs include:

Codeine.

Methadone.

Ritalin.

Schedule I of the Schedule

The drugs in this category are subject to more regulations and fines that are higher than other medications. The program I drugs do not have any medically accepted reputable use , and also have a greater chance of misuse. The kinds of medicines that are included in Timetable I include:

Ecstasy.

Quaaludes.

Don't Allow Drugs Destroy Your Life

It doesn't matter if you or someone you care about is dependent on the Routine V benzodiazepine or an opioid. Dependency is a devastating illness that prevents people from living the life you're supposed to live. Although all types of addiction require special treatment, certain rehabilitation programs can help. Talk to professionals in your field and find the most effective treatment option for you.

Understanding Illegal Drugs

Illicit-drugs are illegal and highly addictive substances like marijuana, heroin and meth. The choice you make for a drug is typically a voluntary one, but quitting once you've been dependent can be a challenge.

A person's drug dependency can affect their mental health and the way they think and perceive things. It also can alter their character and behavior.

The beginning of a drug-related disorder is characterized by a physical dependence on it as well as an increase in tolerance and the results of abuse. Tolerance can occur when you take higher doses of the substance in order to get the same result that you experienced when you first started. If the person is exposed to the facts about the drug, it is possible to rebound if they try to stop. But, there's an urge to stay away from the drug and also to prioritize the use of it over family and relationships.

The symptoms of drawback are serious and can include chest pains and seizures based on the type of drug being used. Drug dependence creates a mental dependence on the drug, this means that the person requires the drug to be in a positive state of mind.

If someone suffering from addiction recognizes the negative side effects of their use of drugs and begins to fight to stay clean. The best method to conquer addiction to illegal substances is to seek seeking treatment in an inpatient rehabilitation facility.

In an inpatient rehabilitation center medical professionals work closely with recovering patients to identify the reason for their drug abuse and any recurrent mental health problems. While in rehab, patients learn effective and healthy ways to will not only assist to keep them off of substances, but also assist them remain content and lead a happy and fulfilled life.

Different types of illegal drugs

If someone in your family or friends has an addiction to drugs there's no reason to feel alone. The study found that 23.9 millions people living in America aged 12 and over around 9.2 percent of the population been using illegal drugs for a few months prior to the study in 2012. Drug use rates are highest among people aged 18-25.

The most commonly used kinds of illicit drugs include:

Cocaine

Cocaine is an extremely stimulant that can be addictive. It is derived from the leaves of South American Coca herb and generally is in the form of powder. Cocaine street names include blow bump, coke and snow. Cocaine is typically snorted or injected. It can also be smoked or applied to the skin.

Crack Cocaine

Crack is the purer and more potent form of cocaine that can be found in crystals or in blocks. Split cocaine is generally taken in a puff and is absorbed into the brain quicker and results in a brief-lived but extremely high-energy. Additionally, it is often administered.

Ecstasy

It is used by numerous high schoolers and adults, it's an ideal party or rave drug. Its psychoactive effects include heightened senses of perception and can cause diminished inhibition. Ecstasy can be taken in pills or in water. However, it is also snorted or inhaled.

Hallucinogens

LSD, PCP, mushrooms and salvias are all types of mind-altering, psychoactive substances While dependence on this drug is more prevalent than other drugs but the misuse and use of the drug may have adverse effects.

Heroin

Heroin is an extremely addictive substance which is extracted from the opium poppy. It's available as the form of a white-brownish or as a dark , sticky component, referred to "dark black tar." It is typically injectable, however it is also consumed in smoke, snorted or consumed.

Inhalants

Inhalants can be found in household products like spray paints, markers, and other cleaning supplies which are inhaled via the nose or mouth to feel energetic or high. Inhaling certain chemicals could cause heart failure and death.

Ketamine

It is commonly used as an anesthetic in vet practice. If misused, ketamine can result in hallucinations, sedation and even confusion.

Marijuana

Cannabis is among the most frequently abused illegal drugs.

The primary psychoactive ingredient, THC, causes short-term feelings of euphoria that are which is accompanied by drowsiness, slow reaction time, and an excessive hunger.

Meth

Meth is a very hazardous stimulant which can lead users to be instantly addicted. The effects meth can have on the user in the short-term include a sense of euphoria and alertness. However, the long-term use of meth could cause issues like aggressive behavior, serious dental hygiene issues psychosis, as well as severe paranoia.

Synthetic Marijuana

Synthetic marijuana is a growing quantity of chemical substances manufactured by humans which contain a chemical component that is identical to THC. Although marijuana manufactured by humans is advertised as legal options but the results of the drug could be unpredictable and more severe than the natural version.

Illegal drug results and abuse

Certain illegal drugs pose significant health risks, even if used in small amounts. Certain drugs may cause dependence following the use. Individuals who are dependent to illegal substances have a higher risk of becoming addicted and death. A lot of overdoses occur when someone relapses following a desire to stop. They believe they require the same treatment as they did before and forget that the body's accustomed to the quantity of medications they use. This is the problem with users who are taking illicit drugs via injection.

Heroin is a drug which can be a source of overdose and relapse. Unfortunately, the amount of deaths linked to opioids, including heroin, has significantly increased over the past 10 years. Between 2002 and 2017, the number of deaths related to opioids increased by more than four times.

The repeated use of illegal drugs could expose the user to both short- and long-term negative consequences. The use of drugs excessively could result in brain damage and can affect your mental well-being. It can cause a person to act out in a strange manner and prompt the person to make self-destructive actions like driving while high.

There are a variety of ways that illegal drugs can adversely affect the person in question:

Disruptions to relationships with families, spouses and family members.

Issues with completing everyday and social responsibilities.

Afraid of from going to work due to the effects of drugs.

A lack of motivation to get excellent grades at school.

The financial burdens resulting from spending money to maintain the habit of using drugs.

Legal consequences, for example, being arrested for a drug offense.

Treatment for Illicit Drug Addiction

If you know someone who suffers from addiction issues There are a variety of alternatives to help them recover and treat. Inpatient as well as outpatient therapy, locating an rehabilitation facility could be the most important step to overcome the addiction disorder. Find out about the treatment options that meet your particular needs.

What exactly is Overdose?

An overdose is a natural reaction your body produces when it encounters a significant amount of substance or a combination of chemicals. It could be a deliberate or accidental. Overdoses can occur from illicit drugs or alcohol, prescription medications as well as other substances. Overdoses can be fatal but a large number of people who overdosed can be saved if help is offered promptly. Overdose is the most common cause of accidents that kill people in America. When it comes to drugs, there are a variety of ways that your body can be overwhelmed by substances. The most prevalent cause of death in any chemical overdose is respiratory failure.

Depressant Overdose

Central nervous system (CNS) include opioids, benzodiazepines and alcohol consumption. These drugs are CNS depressants decrease temperatures and pressure in the blood. It also can slow breathing and heartbeat. This is the reason why these drugs induce sedative effects and cause anxiety and an increased calm and ecstatic effects. If a large quantity of depressants are used this can cause negative effects, like respiratory failure and coma. or even death.

Opioid Overdose

Opioids are among the most natural substances to overdose ondue to how they affect the body when used. Your body produces opioid receptors in various areas that are located in the brain the peripheral and central nervous systems, and the digestive tract. When someone is using opioids these receptors get activated and reduce the body's performance. When your body is overwhelmed by opioids, a number of receptors are blocked and it is unable to perform other tasks. This can lead to an increased chance of overdosing. This could reduce the speed of breathing for a person. Certain opioids can be extremely dangerous in that it may take several minutes for a person who has taken heroin to feel the effects of the overdose. However, a person who is using fentanyl may feel the effects in moments. The powerful and addictive opioids that are why the president of America declared an opioid crisis in the United States in the year 2017.

What exactly is Naloxone?

Naloxone is a vital weapon to fight the overdose of opioids. Naloxone is a popular substance made out of Narcan can be a powerful opioid antagonist which will reduce an opioid's effects on your body. If someone is suffering from an overdose and the condition is serious multiple doses of Narcan will reduce the severity and even save the life of the person. Narcan has no prescription requirements in America.

Alcohol Overdose

An overdose of alcohol occurs when you consume much more than you is able to safely process. In general, your body can absorb around 1 unit of alcohol every hour (approximated to equal what is that is contained in one shot of liquor half-pint of beer (or 1 glass wine).

If someone consumes more alcohol than this in a short time the alcohol will build up in the body since the body can't process the alcohol in a timely manner and the build-up of alcohol is absorbed throughout the body. This can lead to an the overdose of alcohol, also known as poisoning by alcohol.

Signs of poisoning by alcohol include:

Mental confusion.

Vomiting.

Seizures.

Slow breathing.

Breathing irregularity.

Hypothermia and bluish epidermis pallor

Factors that affect your likelihood of suffering from an alcohol-related overdose are:

Age.

Gender.

Body Dimension.

Tolerance.

Binge Drinking

Use of Drugs

Other medical concerns

Other risks that could arise because of drinking higher quantities of alcohol than the body is able to metabolize include:

A slower breathing rate, a gag reflex and a slowing of heartbeat.

Cardiac arrest can be attributed to a reduction in temperatures (hypothermia).

regular seizures due to low blood sugar levels

Stimulant Overdose.

Drugs that stimulate, like cocaine or meth, focus on the CNS However in contrast they can enhance heartbeat and blood circulation pressure body temperature, as well as breathing. The overdose of stimulants happens whenever the heart respiratory system, and the the blood circulation system is exhausted until it wears down.

Signs of a stimulant overdose are:

The limbs are stiff or jerky.

Rapidly rising body temperature or an unexpected burst of high fever.

A rising pulse.

Consciousness loss.

Convulsions, seizures or seizures.

Chest pain.

Headaches that are severe.

Extreme sweating.

Agitation and irritation.

The condition is referred to as mental confusion or disorientation.

Hypertension severe.

Delirium.

Stroke.

Cardiac arrest.

Heart attack.

Atypical or shallow breathing

Certain medications can in reducing or stabilizing symptoms like blood pressure or body temperature, pulse as well as any respiratory condition. There are also medicines that can help people who are experiencing seizures or convulsions like anti-epileptic drugs. If you can get the patient in the hospital of your choice as quickly as possible could save the life of a patient.

Assistance to Treat Overdose

Be aware that treating an overdose at home isn't the same as seeking assistance from an emergency room. Even if the patient appears to be recovering but there's an opportunity that a relapse may be occurring or that something is taking place within the body of the patient that which the patient is not aware of. A visit to a hospital could make significant difference to how long the patient can live or pass away.

The term "overdose" is frightening and is usually linked to death, but it's not always linked to death. It is possible to live a normal life after receiving treatment for an overdose. However, the patient needs to understand the concept and gain knowledge from it.

It's not something that can be achieved quickly, however, it's doable, and not only that, there's an assurance that the patient will never experience an overdose ever again.

If you're not sure of what to do or if you require help for someone you care about, contact a specialist in treatment. They're available all hours of the day, to answer any questions that you might have, whether it's about yourself or for someone else.

Chapter 5: The Reasons People are addicted to Alcohol.

Young and old, men and women and elderly, regardless of the region, age or circumstance, all can become addicted to alcohol.

Anxiety and Stress

The way we live in our current society has a physical impact in every one of us.

Some people are not able to handle the stress. Stress at work, the hours of overtime and home problems are only some of the reasons behind the stress to appear.

Some people drink alcohol to get rid of all this stress and anxiety It's a logical solution but is not a lasting illusion.

One way to ease the stress for many people is to turn to substances that will give the user with some time to relax in which all worries will be resolved.

The quest for alcohol for relaxation doesn't have to happen after work, and neither should it be in the bar. In certain cases there is a situation where the person is not employed and is able to become addicted to drinking alcohol at home in his home.

To have the experience

Drinking with the expectation that it will be enjoyable tend to be more inclined to consume alcohol than those who do not. Therefore, the belief that drinking is enjoyable and fun can lead a person to drink more.

Social pressure

Alcohol is now widely accessible and is aggressively promoted through TV, films advertisements, radio and on the internet. The normalization of alcohol consumption makes it accepted and acceptable particularly in nations or areas where alcohol is an integral aspect of everyday the daily routine.

Factors like the influence of older or parents can influence the initial alcohol consumption. For instance parents who drink more often and view drinking positively could have children who are doing similar.

Most likely, we've felt the same stress throughout our lives. Indeed, nearly everyone is trying to be accepted. A lot of people drink while in a social environment in a place where everybody else is drinking to feel accepted and a part of the group.

Chapter 6: Why Should You Undergo withdrawal and treatment for Alcohol Addiction?

People who would like to stop drinking usually inquire whether there are any advantages in abstaining from drinking. The question is usually requested by those who get an advantage drinking alcohol. The people who drink to forget about their issues or to unwind or relax after a long day, and those who drink to have pleasure have all the excuses to make. But these are just the short-term benefits alcohol can provide. The real advantages of drinking no alcohol:

You'll be feeling better physically and have less medical issues

You'll be more comfortable in your mind and be able to make better decisions and be more efficient in memory retention and cognitive capabilities

You'll be able improve your personal relationships , especially with your spouse as well as your children, partners and the immediate family.

You'll be able to enhance your career, handle projects, oversee your business and become the best you can be in your job and at the classroom.

You can set your personal goals with confidence, but this time you won't need the confidence that comes from bottles.

You'll be able to feel more comfortable, and gone are the worries, depression and guilt of being hard for your loved ones.

You'll be able to enhance your financial situation. Consuming too much alcohol costs money and can drain your bank account when you're not careful.

You'll be able avoid other actions that are associated with drinking, such as taking gambling, drugs, sexual addiction, and so on.

You'll enjoy more time playing and be a good friend to those you cherish. You can make plans for the future of your family as you make wise decisions that benefit your family and you in the near future.

You'll be able to assist others to overcome their own alcohol addiction. Individuals who have succeeded in recovering from addiction issues are encouraged to become counselors and associates for those who are just beginning their journey. You'll be an inspirational role model and excellent role model for other people.

Chapter 7: Understanding Alcoholism

It's not always easy to know if your drinking habit has shifted from moderate or social drink to alcohol abuse. One method to determine whether you're already in a danger zone is when you consume alcohol to manage issues or are trying to avoid negative feelings. Alcoholism is a process that slowly takes over your life, and it is essential to be aware of the warning signs , so you can take the appropriate actions to curb your alcohol consumption once you realize there are indications. The first step towards overcoming alcoholism is to comprehend it.

The causes of addiction to alcohol are many interconnected factors like the person's genetics, how they was raised, the environment that you reside in and your psychological situation. Based on research that have identified certain ethnic groups like those of Native Alaskan and the American Indian that are more at risk of being dependent on alcohol as compared to other groups. If alcoholism is a common occurrence within your family or you are closely associated with others who drink heavily there is a greater chance of developing issues when it comes to drinking. Additionally, if suffering from a mental illness like depression, bipolar disorder or anxiety, you're most likely to be at risk because you might be highly tempted to drink alcohol for self-medication.

Because drinking alcohol is common in many societies and its effects vary widely between people It is often difficult to tell if an individual is at the point of having a drink in a club, and an alcohol abuser. In the final analysis, it is important to inquire about how alcohol impacts your life. If your drinking habits are leading to problems within your life, then it is likely that you have drinking issues.

The signs and symptoms

As a professional in substance abuse There is a distinct difference between alcoholism and abuse. An alcoholic is one who you're in general depended on drinking alcohol. You may not go for a day, or even just a few hours, without drinking. However you're an addict if you possess the ability to place some restrictions on your drinking habits, but your drinking habits are considered to be harmful and self-destructive, not just to you but also to others and to the general public. Here are a few of the most frequently observed symptoms and indicators of being an alcoholic:

The habit of drinking causes you to frequently ignore your obligations at home or at work. You always arrive late to work, or even worse than that, you don't go to work completely. You don't pay attention to your children and skip important events due to suffering from an alcohol-related hangover.

It is possible to drink alcohol in situations that could pose physical risk to you as well as others. It happens whenever you are driving drunk and or operate machines even though you're under the influence or mix alcoholic drinks with prescribed drugs in contradiction to the advice of your physician.

There are legal issues that you face repeatedly due to your drinking habits. This is the reason you are constantly taken into custody for DUI or for drunk or inconsiderate behavior.

It is okay to continue drinking the alcohol consumption is already creating problems in your relationships at work and in your personal life. It happens when you continue drinking with your friends even though you know that your wife is upset by your behavior or when you argue with others in your family because they continue to tell you that they are not happy with your behavior when you're drunk.

Drinking alcohol is a method of relaxation or for de-stressing. Many people begin drinking disorders when they drink alcohol in order to calm themselves and lower their stress. This is the case when you decide to drink after a long and tiring day or whenever you are in a dispute with your spouse.

Denial

This is among the biggest obstacles to getting help for your addiction to alcohol. Your urge to consume alcohol is so intense that your brain can come up with many ways to justify drinking alcohol, even when the adverse effects are very evident. Denying your drinking causes more issues because it prevents you from examining how you act and the negative results which result from your actions. Here are some of the ways you might be denying the drinking problem:

You are wildly underestimating the amount of alcohol you consume.

You minimize the harmful consequences of drinking.

You are complaining that your loved ones overstate the drinking problem.

The blame falls on other people for your drinking problems and the challenges you confront due to it. You might blame your boss of not being fair or your spouse for making you feel naive instead of taking a look at the way your drinking habits contribute to the problem. We all face the same pressures from our families and work. If you've noticed a pattern of getting worse due to these pressures, and you constantly blame other people this could be a sign that you are struggling with alcohol.

If you realize that you constantly justify your drinking habits or tell people you are lying about it, or refuse to discuss the subject It is recommended for you to take a moment to think about the reasons behind being so defensive. If you are certain that you don't have any issues with drinking there is no reason for you to cover up anything regarding your drinking practices.

Steps to Start Your Recovery

Beating your addiction to alcohol can be a long and challenging process. There will be times where you feel it's impossible to overcome your addiction. It is important to believe that it's not impossible as many others have made it happen before you. If you're prepared to stop drinking and are ready to receive the assistance you need, you'll be able to recover from the effects of alcohol addiction, regardless of how severe your condition is or how insignificant you believe you are. It is not necessary to delay your recovery plan until you've reached the point of no return. You are able to begin your journey at any time. The subsequent chapters will guide you through the steps to begin the journey towards the end of alcohol today.

Chapter 8: Starting the Sober Journey Safely

Once you have set your goals and plans, you're now ready to begin your journey to a sober life. While a lot of individuals will require the assistance of medical attention and guidance to stop drinking, some are able to make it happen independently. The best option for you is contingent on the duration of time, frequency and amount of alcohol you consume. If you suffer from health problems related to drinking, it's recommended to consult a doctor and health-related treatment. The only thing we're always aching for and yearning to do is live a life in a manner that is healthy and safe.

According to health science research, the body of an individual becomes dependent on alcohol when they drink often and regularly. This means that you'll become physically dependent on substances which are related to alcohol. The withdrawal symptoms include:

Shaking,

Sweating,

Nausea or vomiting,

Headaches,

An increase in blood pressure or an increase in heart rate

Sleep problems and concentration issues,

Stress and anxiety, and

Stomach cramps and diarrhea.

The majority of the time, these symptoms last between five to one week if you're not a regular drinker. However, for people who have been drinking often throughout their lives, the effects can end up costing their lives, as circumstances generally aren't pleasant. The following scenarios could be apparent:

Confusion and disorientation

Severe vomiting

Fever

Convulsions or seizures

Hallucinations

Extremely high exaggerated agitation

The symptoms described above occur from the withdrawal of alcohol that is extreme. It could be due to the condition called the DTs or Delirium Tremens. Very rarely will you meet people suffering from this condition, but should you become a victim to it during the process, seeking urgent medical consultation will offer you the highest level of treatment. It could be connected with changes in the circulation of blood, as well as breathing.

In case you've been drinking all of your life , pursuing an Detox program will give you the best results. This program is available in the hospital, as an outpatient or in a center to treat alcohol addiction. This is the most preferred option for people who are heavy drinkers. The process involves an medical prescription to keep you from any complications or signs related to the withdrawal process and the decision to quit.

Chapter 9: Tips and Tricks to successfully stop drinking Alcohol

Tips and Recommendations

Have you been contemplating the need to stop drinking? Are you concerned about the negative effects of drinking alcohol on your health and relationships? Are you pondering whether alcohol is helping your health or hurting it? If these are the thoughts in your mind and you're not sure, then look into stopping drinking. As most people believe, it's not to late. In reality many have changed their lives by opting to become sober. So, you're not an the only one.

It does not matter what you've gone through during your time with alcohol. Don't dwell over what you've done up to now. Most important is that you're ready and ready to take the first step towards sobriety. Therefore, you should focus on the positive things that are coming your way. A large part of your recovery depends on your attitude towards the issue. Therefore, it is essential that you establish an optimistic mindset that says everything will be fine at the end. If you can believe that with this mindset you'll be able to keep striving despite the difficulties you'll encounter.

This chapter offers an extensive guideline on how to stop drinking. The advice here can help you overcome common challenges faced by addicts on their journey to recovery.

Acknowledge the Issue

The first step in achieving sobriety is to admit you're an alcohol addict. Before thinking about any other options you must first acknowledge that you are suffering from an issue and require help from a professional. The most interesting aspect of drinking is that people are constantly in a state of confusion about their drinking habits. Many people aren't sure if they are addicts or regular drinking people. Finding yourself in the gray zone is the most awful thing that could occur to you. It is because of the fact that you may not think you'll need assistance. In most cases, you drink heavily thinking you're in control. However, as the habit of drinking takes root it can be difficult to reverse.

If you notice that you're often between thoughts and not knowing if you're more successful than your peers or people who consume alcohol heavily. Additionally, you may be tempted to take part in online assessments to discover whether you're dependent or not. If that's the scenario, you should consider taking the steps listed below.

Be Prepared to Answer the right questions

A lot of times, we pay our attention on the negative aspects and overlook the fact the fact that we are heavily dependent on the mindset we adopt. People are prone to believe that they are immune to all negative events that occur to them. In the case of drinking, people will constantly question whether they are addicted or not. If you continue asking yourself this question there is a good chance you're an addict. You're worried about the direction your life is heading. You may have developed a pattern that can cause you to worry.

Instead of thinking about the negative side of your drinking you need to consider whether your drinking habits are preventing your ability to live the life that you'd hoped to live. Perhaps it's preventing you from spending the time with your family. Perhaps alcohol is causing problems with your coworkers. Therefore, you should consider your own thoughts about the impact alcohol has in your personal life. If it's keeping you the ability to live your life, acknowledge that it is. This is an initial step.

Stop Comparing Yourself to Other People

As an addict who has a history of alcohol dependence I can admit that there are occasions that you take a moment to think about how you compare yourself to others are drinking with. In reality, there's no benefit from this. Actually, it can lead to a situation where it is easier to justify drinking habits. Instead of realizing you are in trouble and resolving it, you convince yourself by saying that you're no worse that the Mr. White down the street.

It is crucial to remember that you live lifestyle in a unique way. You are your own and, therefore it is important to look within yourself and not compare your life to others. If you're struggling with an addiction to alcohol, you must admit it. You're different from the Mr. White and your body tolerance levels are different. Remember this drinking alcohol, you're not harming another person's body, but rather your own. Therefore, avoid comparing your self to other people.

Take a moment to think about your future

In the same manner as the drinking habits that you've established, think on what you want to be five years from now. Are you satisfied with your new self? If not, then you're suffering from an addiction to alcohol. You're certain that you are suffering from an alcohol addiction however you're not willing to admit that you have a problem. Do not remain in the dark. Pick the right path to begin your journey towards healing.

Learn the Reasons You Should Stop drinking

Congratulations for taking that first step and admitting you require assistance in regaining your health and living a an alcohol-free life. The next thing to be searching at is motivation. You may be able to admit that you need to cut down on drinking, but what? If you aren't motivated to make the decision, then you won't be compelled to make the change.

Most people think that the best method to get yourself motivated is making a list of the benefits to your health that you'll be enjoying when you stop drinking. This isn't the best strategy to be effective over the long term. Consider the short-term benefits that appear once you quit drinking. These short-term advantages can help you understand that it is indeed possible to benefit from altering your habits. Thus the benefits could include the following.

Reclaim Lost Time

We are usually compelled to believe that drinking on the weekend isn't an effective way to kill time. In the end, you've been working all week. Therefore drinking for a few hours is not a bad thing. You could be mistaken. If you consume alcohol for the equivalent of 3 hours each weekend with your group of friends, that means you will lose around 12 hours over the course of the course of a month. In the course of a year, you'll lose 6 days. It's just an equation to help to realize that you spend lots of time by drinking alcohol. Therefore, if you choose instead to not drink the immediate reward will be the chance to reclaim this time to utilize it to your advantage.

Get Rich Quickly

If you're an addicted person, paying $200 each weekend isn't a huge issue. Self-justification is going to convince you you're giving yourself a reward for your hard-earned cash. But the truth is that you're simply poisoning yourself. After years of drinking, you can be sure that you'll have to have to spend more money to heal yourself and get back from the addiction. So, be sure to motivate yourself to save the money for more productive motives.

Sleep More Soundly

As was previously stated it is not a good idea to believe the belief that having one before bed will assist you in getting to sleep. Being a depressant, alcohol can just negatively impact your sleeping patterns. This means that you'll feel exhausted every time you get up. This is because your body doesn't get the rest it needs. The decision to stop drinking will also improve the quality of sleep that you receive.

Engage in more meaningful conversations

One of the immediate benefits you'll gain from abstaining from alcohol is that you'll find it easy to talk to people. When you talk to people while drunk can sever from the genuineness of your conversations. People will never pay attention to the words you speak because it's not your real voice talking. The consequence of being addicted to alcohol is that you'll be less likely to speak with others when you're sober. So, you must realize the importance of engaging in meaningful conversations with others.

In all likelihood, there are numerous reasons you shouldn't drink. It is crucial to recognize this fact in order to encourage you to continue in your pursuit of sobriety. This will assist you in dealing with the numerous questions that could be on your mind regarding living a sober lifestyle. It is not a time to live in the dark because you're confident of the advantages that you'll get by staying sober. In this way, you'll be motivated to take every step with confidence.

Prioritize the cause

If you are struggling with addiction, the main thing you should keep in your head is to get back control over your life. This is definitely the only thing you need to be doing throughout the process of recovery. You had provided your friend with a motive to be the best out of you. Accept your mistakes and choose not to follow the same direction over and over again.

The aim of stopping drinking should be the first priority in everything you undertake. Make a set of ground rules to remind you of the have to remain focussed. Do not enter any social gatherings in which you may be attracted. Don't listen to the voice in on the back of your head affirming that one glass of wine isn't going to harm you. Make sure you are focusing on the cause from the beginning to conclusion. In the end, you'll be content that you decided to pursue the road that leads to happiness and a lifetime of health.

Beware of Drinking Friends

When you try to find ways to get rid of your drinking habits and you are told to keep your drinking buddies away from you. This isn't something that is easy to accomplish. Eliminating all your acquaintances will appear impossible. But you must recognize that getting over your addiction isn't easy if you surround yourself with those who drink. If it's your friends or family members it is important to make them aware that you're trying to end your addiction. No matter how silly you be in front of your friends who have known you for a while but just let it be known.

Another step you must take is to avoid friends who the only connection you shared was drinking. If all you could think regarding your buddy was seeing drunk and a few beers, there's nothing wrong with removing them from your Facebook account. You must realize that the friendship you had wasn't productive.

Certainly it is true that leaving these friends isn't easy. It is nevertheless essential to surround yourself with people who can aid you in your recovery. Now is the best time to meet new people. Get connected with those who train regularly and remind them why it is important to work out every day. They can assist you in detoxing and help you schedule other activities that are more enjoyable.

Be Proud of Your Goals

It is crucial to emphasize on the reasons you need to make your decisions that you will make from this point to the next. Your family and friends should know that you've decided to end your drinking. Sure, they'll be a bit irritated at first but they will soon realize that you're doing it to fulfill a noble purpose. In addition, they'll start to notice a shift in you and want to celebrate with them. The reason you should be able to share your story to the people who are around you is to assist in making sure that you're in the right direction. Consider it this way when your friend is thinking about inviting you for a gathering with drinks, they'll be cautious because they are aware that you shouldn't be at risk. Therefore, you are helping yourself by telling others about the choices you're making in your daily life.

Recognize the withdrawal symptoms

A crucial part of recovery is to be aware of the unpleasantness of withdrawal symptoms you'll encounter. If you're an alcohol addict, these withdrawal symptoms could be your most terrifying nightmare. It is important not to be scared of the whole process. But, it is essential to be prepared for the challenges that lie ahead. The first few days of alcohol-free is going to be a painful experience. It will be as if you've gone for three days without eating. The cravings will be overwhelming. This is the primary reason why you must seek help from a professional. Even in spite of your difficult experiences, you must realize that the advantages of stopping drinking alcohol outnumber the reasons you shouldn't drink.

Some of the signs you may experience are the occurrence of tremors, insomnia and elevated temperatures, excessive sweating seizures, tremors, elevated blood pressure. These symptoms should signal that your body is on a quest to detox its body naturally. Naturally, you'll be inclined to drink alcohol to ease the discomfort you feel. But this could cause the possibility of a rebound. This is an excellent reason to need to seek professional help. They can guide you on the correct medication to take to aid your body in its detox without causing any discomfort.

Change Your Attitude

It is inevitable that you'll occasionally be defensive time. Whatever the case, you need to modify your mindset towards the situation you're in. The medical professionals will pressure you to do something that you don't like. Be prepared for this test and know that everything is done to aid you in recovering. Within you it is crucial to not feel like you're losing due to what has happened to you. Remember that what happened you was in the past. Sure, you may have suffered a loss however the most important thing to remember is that you're blessed to live a full life. Consider the significance of the decision you've made to live in a clean and healthy life. Recognize this. Avoid focusing on the negative events that happened because it will drain your energy needed to focus on getting back to your normal.

Undoubtedly, it will not be easy to cultivate an optimistic mindset in the face of all you're experiencing is a challenging circumstance. But, try to realize that getting your recovery in an appropriate angle is the most effective method of making sure you get through the process smoothly.

Check into a Rehabilitation Center

It's true that there are times when it's next to impossible to get yourself from drinking. It is difficult to be able to discern the best steps that you can take to get back to health. That's why you must seek help from a professional. You could opt for either outpatient or inpatient programs to aid you in overcoming your illness.

Before you decide on a program it is important to review the services provided by various facilities. This ensures that you go for the one that best fits your lifestyle and degree of addiction. In some instances it is a choice to be taken by your family members. You can let them help you. Do not be angry about the whole process. Try convincing yourself that they're doing all they can to save your life from the past. Why? It's not because they're rich and they cherish you enough to help you live a healthy as well.

Chapter 10: Committing To Change

The issue of alcohol addiction which affects a significant proportion of people and can take hold of you with no warning. The physical signs may be evident, like confusion, slurred speech nausea, and loss consciousness. Sometimes an individual is a victim of alcohol addiction with no warning signs, that make it more difficult to overcome. People can drink throughout the day and still function well in the world of everyday life and so they can fool everybody around them. Is this a reason to be able to live in peace? No, it's not. What's going on inside might not be visible on the outside, however in the near future, the body's systems will begin to slow down and the possibility of permanent injury increases.

Alcohol is one of the most difficult addictions to overcome since our culture is one of culture where drinking is seen as an essential component of having enjoyable.

However, when you cross the line between moderate and social drinking into regular drinking, you'll know you're in the zone of danger. If you're reading this, you're likely aware that you may have a problem, regardless of whether someone else has warned you about that or if you've come to recognize yourself. It is possible, however, that you remain living in denial. If that is the case, you must be honest with yourself:

Do you drink alcohol every day?

Do you tell lies to your friends about your drinking habits?

Do you think you're in need of a drink alcohol to be more comfortable?

Have you heard of anyone who could be concerned about you?

Do you often forget about your work or your home due to drinking?

Do you depend on your drink to perform on a regular basis?

Do you require more alcohol than you did for the sake of feeling drunk?

When you aren't drinking, do you experience anxiety or depressed?

Do you still drink despite knowing it's causing you problems?

Are any of the above sounds familiar to you?

Alcoholism can sneak up over time. It's not common to want to be addicted However, it develops gradually and without any warning. The process may be so gradual that you do not even notice the process taking place. The problem is that you've built up an aversion to it that you are more at ease and feel more yourself when you drink than when you aren't.

As with every addiction, you're not all on your own. With determination and a sense of humour, you can conquer it, and you can.

All you need is to make the commitment to changes.

Chapter 11: Alter the way you drink

If a person has changed the way that he/she lives, it's the right time to make changes to the way in which he or she consumes alcohol. This is crucial as the way in which one drinks needs to be changed in order to stop the misuse of alcohol, and especially because they cannot guarantee that they will never or she consume alcohol again at any time in the near future. They must be aware or be taught the correct ways to drink alcohol and ensure that they are in control every time they drink alcohol. The time will come when they'll sit before a glass of alcohol and wonder what they are supposed to conduct their lives. If they haven't been taught how to properly drink alcohol The old habits will return and the dependence and abuse will take over their lives and bring back the same problems they believed were a thing of the past.

It's been widely accepted that something that's a part of one's life is not able to be completely erased with one swipe. Instead, it should be eliminated from his or her life, in small steps. If this is a case of alcohol dependence and the person normally drinks alcohol, lets say, two times a week, then the initial step is to drink the drink only once per week for a month. Once you have taken it for every week for a month, it's time to drink it 10 days for a month. After having it taken every 10 days over the course of a month it's high time to only take it once a month, every two weeks. If you are taking it two times a month, it's high time that they should only take it every month... and reduce the amount again over and over until they be drinking alcohol at, say, at least every three or four months. At some point, the person will see that they was not drinking in alcohol for the entire year, as he/she took it in a gradual manner without thinking about the implications about their goal. In all of this instances, it's clear that in the battle against addiction to alcohol, the best way is not to eradicate the problem once and for all however, it is to decrease the amount of alcohol consumed slowly until drinking alcohol occurs just once or twice per year. Also, individuals should learn how to drink responsibly, not to stop completely drinking, but rather to drink alcohol in a manner that is safe for them.

However when trying to conquer drinking, it is recommended to reduce the amount they drink by tiny. If, for instance, one typically consumes eight bottles of alcohol during one drink, the first step is to reduce the number of bottles down to six such as. The next step is to reduce it by four bottles. The third step is decreasing it further to three bottles until they can only drink only two bottles during one drink. Similar to the way, the best approach isn't to completely eliminate the consumption from alcohol. The goal is instead to reduce the amount consumed slowly taking one step at one step at a time. Consider it as a step by little to avoid becoming overwhelmed by the goal of reducing the consumption of alcohol.

It is also vital that anyone who is seeking to conquer alcohol abuse and addiction be capable of identifying the areas of danger the best time and place to be likely to consume alcohol. They should avoid by doing other activities or going to different places and not being in the danger zones during those most risky moments during the course of the day. If, for instance, that the zone of danger is 7 pm , after the day has ended and the work has been done, it will be safer to perform breathing exercises at this period of time. This can help them avoid being impacted by the consequences of not drinking alcohol during that particular time during the course of their day. You can also do some yoga or other relaxation exercises in the comfort of their own home.

If the danger zone is located at the residence of a person is a frequent stop on their way back to work, it's high time to take a different route to get back to work. Experts have stated that overcoming the moment of impulse by two or three times could eventually result in a zero desire, to the point that there is no reason to consume any substance. It is not necessary to be strong all day long. It is enough to be aware of what their weaknesses and strengths are and also the times and places that they are more likely to feel pushed or prompted to drink the alcohol. They must be aware of their risk zones, so that they can be prepared to confront them with appropriate strategies. Something that is not compatible with addiction as anything that is difficult to overcome, like alcohol, must be battled over. That means that they must be ready to confront them one by one, particularly at the worst period of the day when they are compelled to go back to the ritual and drink. Sometimes it is possible to take a break however this should only be done when there's nothing to be done, and there is nothing to quell the craving to have a taste alcohol.

Chapter 12: Online Support Group

There is lots of support and support through support groups on the internet. The internet offers many options of assistance for those trying to cut down on drinking or if you are trying to get rid of any other addictive or harmful habits. There are lots of different kinds of support groups that you can find online with groups specifically designed for people who are determined to get off the booze for good.

Online support groups are far more convenient than other groups since you can join the online meetings without leaving the comforts of home. If you own an internet camera, you could provide the online meetings with a more intimate experience.

Online support groups aren't difficult to locate at all. You can conduct a lookup on your favorite search engine for online support groups for AA and online AA support and so on. A myriad of groups will likely pop up. The most well-known and popular groups will be close to on the search results. Then, you can do some study on those groups that you are interested in most and choose which one(s) you'd like to explore.

The majority of online support groups are organized , and like other groups, they've scheduled weeks, days beginning and ending times and a moderator within the chat room in the group that usually decides on the chat room's theme. Along with the setting of the chatroom's subject they also set the topic of the support group's online moderators of chat rooms also oversee the activity in the chatroom and can answer any questions chat room members might have.

Online support groups can be an excellent option for people who feel shy or are worried about meeting many people to receive some assistance from those who can relate to their circumstances. The internet can be a great way to connect with people who have similar experiences and provide you with assistance and help.

If you're trying to quit drinking or consuming alcohol, it's beneficial to be able connect with others who know the issues you're facing and who are experiencing the same challenges. Support groups on the internet provide the opportunity to do this. Finding a reliable online support group is a great component of your recovery.

Chapter 13: What is Drug Classification?

Drug classifications help categorize the drugs into categories.

The classification of drugs based on similarities to substances is essential because chemically related drugs can have similar influences and dangers. Anyone who is dependent on a substance will likely misuse it, and may rely on a different drug which is chemically related. In spite of these generalities, chemically identical drugs could be different in terms of legal and medical consequences.

There are many ways to classify substances based on their effects on the body and brain such as, for instance, certain drugs can make one feel vigorous and energetic, while others give more tranquility.

The majority of countries have a legal class system of drugs. These classification systems define the conditions that the drug is legal, if there are any, which the drug is legally legal as well as the different requirements that must be met for the drug, as well as any legal penalties associated to distribution, ownership, or its manufacturing. Legal classifications typically are determined by the therapeutic value of the drug as well as its known risks.

There is a debate about the way that drugs should be classified and even among experts. This means that the same drug could be classified in two different groups with similar names. Because of these differences it is impossible to create the "definitive" group of classifications for drugs.

Drug Classifications Based On Chemical Makeup

Alcohol

Alcohol is the most misused substance around the globe which includes in the U.S. Alcohols have a significant impact on many bodily systems that creates a variety of risks for those who drink it. Consuming alcohol triggers feelings of euphoria that decrease inhibitions. It also results in visual impairment. Alcohols are a central nervous system depressant. It causes the most painful long-term damage in the liver. There are a variety of forms of drinking alcohol, which include:

Beer.

Wine.

Liquor.

Opioids

Opioids, also referred to as opiates, can be made from opium or are chemical compounds created to imitate the effects of it. Opioids function by interfering with heart neurotransmitters and block the signals they transmit. They can serve as powerful painkillers, but they also provide extreme pleasure, which can lead to dependence. Opioid addiction is among the most serious issues faced in America currently. They are among the most addictive of the chemicals that are known and among the most deadly. The most well-known opioids are:

Heroin.

Fentanyl.

Oxycodone.

Benzodiazepines

Benzodiazepines or Benzos are a category of medications that function by interfering with the neurotransmitter, gamma-aminobutyric acid (GABA-A). The individual Benzo works with GABA-A a variety of ways, which is the reason each Benzo impacts the brain and body in a different way. Benzos are suggested to manage various mental and physical conditions but they are frequently misused. Benzos are extremely addicting and could cause many mental and medical issues. The types of Benzos include:

Ativan.

Valium.

Xanax.

Cannabinoids

Cannabinoids are a class of substances which are chemically related with tetrahydrocannabinol (THC) which is the active ingredient in marijuana. Cannabinoids generate feelings of joy However, they negatively affect physical and mental health. Cannabinoids are among the most frequently used and abused drug after alcohol, and are getting increasingly legal approval. Though they are less harmful than other drug classifications, cannabinoids could significantly impact a person's mental and physical health. The types of cannabinoids are:

Marijuana.

Hashish.

Barbiturates

Barbiturates impede the function that the brain and central nervous system performs. they are the derivatives of the chemical barbituric acidity. Barbiturates have been used for centuries in treating sleep disorders and psychiatric disorders as well as anesthesia, and other ailments like epilepsy and headache. Barbiturates are extremely addictive and have a significant likelihood of being a victim of an overdose since they can trigger several systems within the body to stop functioning.

The types of barbiturates that are available include:

Amytal.

Luminal.

Pentobarbital.

The classification of Drugs based on Effects

Depressants

Also known in the context of "downers," depressants create feelings of tiredness and relaxation. Although many have legitimate goals such as combating insomnia and mental disorders however, they are often misused because they can induce feelings of happiness. Depression isn't just one of the drugs that are highly addictive; they're also among the most dangerous and likely to lead to an overdose. The types of depressants are:

Alcohol.

Opiates.

Barbiturates.

Stimulants

Also called "uppers," the first purpose of stimulants is to boost concentration, energy and alertness. They are believed to trigger the sensation of a energy rush i.e an energy boost. Since a certain time they are believed to enhance performance and efficiency, as well as evoking satisfaction. As time passes, stimulants can become extremely addictive and have an extremely high chance of misuse. Some types of stimulants include:

Adderall.

Cocaine.

Meth.

Hallucinogens

Hallucinogens, sometimes referred to as dissociative affect the user's perception of reality and can cause visual and auditory hallucinations often referred to by the term "tripping." While hallucinogens can be less dependent than other classifications of drugs but they're generally more severe and risky. Some hallucinogens are:

LSD.

Psilocybin Mushrooms.

PCP.

Inhalants

Inhalants comprise a wide range of chemicals that are consumed most often by breathing them into or puffing. Inhalants are mostly used substances which are not suitable for human consumption. Because there's a variety of inhalants, they all result in feelings of energy and increased. Inhalants aren't studied as extensively as other substances; however, while they're generally less addictive compared to other substances however, inhalation is risky and can cause negative health issues. Commonly abused inhalants are:

Paint thinner.

Remove polish from your toenails.

Gasoline

The Federal government adopted The Controlled Chemicals Do Something Act in 1970 as a response to the rising drug problem. The legislation established five classifications for drugs. What uses a substance is determined by its legitimacy and possible medical applications, in conjunction with the possibility of addiction and addiction. America must categorize the use of specific substances using schedules in order to adhere to agreements with diplomatic institutions, such as that of the Single Convention on Narcotic Drugs.

Schedule V

The drugs in the Program V class have the smallest regulations and have the most affordable penalties of any classification. The Plan V drugs are the most medically accepted use, and have a lower risk of misuse over Timetable IV drugs, and offer a less risk of becoming addicts in comparison to Schedule IV drugs. For example:

Lomotil.

Motoren.

Lyrica

Schedule IV

Plan IV drugs have regulations and fines for Timetable V and Routine III drugs. Plan IV drugs have the highest known medical use, the least chance of abuse; and a low risk of craving. For example:

Ambien.

Darvocet.

Tramadol

Schedule III

Schedule III drugs have higher rules and fines that are more severe in comparison to Regular IV drugs and fewer rules and fewer severe penalties in comparison to Plan II drugs. Schedule III drugs are categorized as having the most effective medical benefits with a lesser risk of abuse than Regimen II and I medications; in addition, they have a lower chance of becoming addicted. The types that belong to Plan III drugs include:

Anabolic steroids.

Ketamine.

Vicodin.

Schedule II

Schedule II drugs are subject to more regulations and stricter penalties than other drug, aside from Regular We drugs. The Plan II drugs have the highest medical benefits, but they also have a higher risk of abuse and a high dependence risk. The types that are part of Timetable II drugs include:

Codeine.

Methadone.

Ritalin.

Schedule I of the Schedule

The drugs in this category are subject to stricter rules and penalties than any other drug. The drugs in the program I category don't contain any approved medical use , and therefore have a greater chance of misuse. The kinds of medicines included in Timetable I include:

Ecstasy.

Quaaludes.

Don't let Drugs ruin your life

It doesn't matter if you or someone you care about is dependent on an Routine V benzodiazepine or an opioid. Dependency is an extremely harmful problem that hinders you from living the kind of life you're supposed to live. Although all types of addiction require special treatment, certain rehabilitation programs can help. Talk to specialists in this field in order to determine the best treatment options for you.

Understanding Illegal Drugs

Illicit-drugs are illegal and highly addictive substances such as heroin meth, marijuana, or. The choice you make for a drug is typically a voluntary one, but stopping once you've become addicted can be difficult.

A person's drug dependency can affect their mental health and the way they think and perceive things. It also can change their behavior and character.

The beginning of a drug-related disorder is characterized by physical dependence to it, tolerance to the drug, and consequences of misuse. Tolerance can occur when you take higher doses of the substance in order to achieve the same effects that you experienced when you first started. If the user is confronted with certain facts about the drug, it could be possible for them to fall back when they attempt to stop. But, there's the desire to not use the drug and also to prioritize the use of it over family and relationships.

In severe cases, the symptoms of drawback can include chest pains and seizures, depending on the type of drug being used. Drug addiction creates a psychological dependence on the drug, this means that the user requires the drug to be in a good state of mind.

When someone suffering from substance abuse begins to realize the negative side effects of their addiction and begins to fight to get rid of it. The most effective way to break addiction to illicit drugs is through the treatment offered by an inpatient rehabilitation facility.

In an inpatient rehabilitation center medical professionals work with recovering patients to identify the reason for their addiction to drugs or recurrent mental health problems. While in rehab, patients learn efficient and healthy methods that will not only assist them stay away from drugs , but also aid them remain content and lead a happy and satisfying life.

Different types of illegal drugs

If someone in your family or friends suffers from an addiction to drugs there's no reason to feel alone. Around 23.9 million individuals in America who are 12 or older roughly 9.2 percent of the population been using illegal drugs for a few months prior to the study in 2012. The rates of using illegal drugs are highest among people aged between 18 and 25.

The most commonly used kinds of illegal drugs include:

Cocaine

Cocaine is an extremely stimulant that is addictive. It is made from the leaves of South American Coca herb and typically is available in powder form. The street names for cocaine are blow bump, coke and snow. Cocaine is usually snorted or injected. It can also be smoked or applied through the skin.

Crack Cocaine

Crack is the purest and most potent version of cocaine. It can be found in crystals or in blocks. Split cocaine is generally taken in a puff and is absorbed into the brain quicker and results in a short-lived , but extremely high-energy. Additionally, it is often injectable.

Ecstasy

Utilized by a lot of high schoolers as well as adults, it's an ideal party or rave drug. Its psychoactive effects include heightened sensations and diminished inhibition. Ecstasy can be taken in form of pills or dissolving in water. It can also be snorted , or injectable.

Hallucinogens

LSD, PCP, mushrooms and salvias are examples of psychoactive , mind-altering drugs. While dependence on this substance is not as prevalent than other drugs however, abuse and use of the drug may result in adverse consequences.

Heroin

Heroin can be a very addictive chemical which is extracted from the opium poppy. It's available in powder form, either white or brown, or in a dark and sticky component, referred to "dark Tar." It is typically inhaled, but it is also available to be taken in the form of smoke, snort or consumed.

Inhalants

Inhalants are household items like spray paints, markers, and cleaning products which are inhaled via the nose or mouth to feel energetic or high. Inhaling certain kinds of chemicals could cause heart failure and death.

Ketamine

It is used in medicine to treat veterinary anesthetic practice. If misused, ketamine can cause hallucinations, sedation and even confusion.

Marijuana

Cannabis is among the most commonly used illegal drugs.

The psychoactive component that is the most prominent, THC, causes short-term feeling of euphoria. It is which is accompanied by drowsiness, slow reaction time, and an excessive hunger.

Meth

Meth is a highly dangerous stimulant that can cause users to develop a rapid addiction. The effects meth can have on the user in the short-term include euphoria and alertness. However, the long-term use of meth could cause issues like aggressive behavior, serious dental hygiene issues psychosis, and extreme paranoia.

Synthetic Marijuana

Synthetic marijuana has a rising amount of synthetic substances that have a chemical substance similar to THC. While marijuana that is made by humans is promoted as a legal choice but the results of the drug could be unpredictable and more intense than its natural counterpart.

Illegal drug results and abuse

A lot of illegal drugs pose serious health risks, even if they are taken in small amounts. Certain drugs can cause dependence following consumption. People who develop dependence on illicit drugs are more at risk of overdosing. This could be fatal. A lot of overdoses occur when an individual relapses when they want to end their addiction. They believe that they require the same treatment they received previously and forget that the body's accustomed to the amount of medications they use. This is the issue for people who use illicit drugs via injection.

Heroin is a substance that is a risk of overdose and relapse. Unfortunately, the amount of deaths linked to opioids, including heroin, has significantly increased over the past 10 years. From 2002 until 2017, the number of opioid-related deaths increased by over four times.

Regular use of illegal substances could expose the user to both short- and long-term negative consequences. In excess, drug use may result in brain damage and can affect your mental well-being. It can cause a person to act out in a strange manner and prompt the person to make self-destructive actions like driving when high.

There are a variety of ways that illegal drugs can adversely affect an individual:

The damage to relationships between families, spouses and even friends.

Troubles in completing the daily and social obligations.

Inability to finish work on time or working due to the effects of drugs.

A lack of motivation to get good grades at school.

Financial difficulties due to the need to spend money to maintain an addiction to drugs.

Legal consequences, like being arrested for drug possession.

Treatment for Illegal Drug Addiction

If you know someone who is struggling with addiction to illegal substances There are a variety of choices to help them recover and treat. If you decide to go through inpatient and outpatient treatments, locating an rehabilitation facility could be the most important step to overcome addiction disorder. Find out about the treatment options that meet the specific needs of your.

Chapter 14: Create Goals and Be Kind To Yourself

Do you have a goal to set for yourself? Is it not difficult! Be consistent and learn patience and striving towards them even if the process takes months, or even years? Much more difficult.

Two things are essential in helping you reach your goals, while remaining determined to achieve them! In this section I'll be discussing the objective of quitting drinking, naturally however, this advice can be applicable to any goal that you set for yourself.

How do you stay motivated?

It's extremely difficult. Motivation can change according to your feelings and what you want to accomplish instead and the events that are happening within your own life in the moment. How do you on Earth do you stay focused, no matter what else going on around you?

Here are some suggestions:

Remember your objectives. This could help remind you why you chose to quit from drinking alcohol in the first in the first. The idea of reliving the amount of time it's going to be to get there can aid in gaining more enthusiasm.

Keep track of your goals. Sometimes it's much more real if you're tracking your goals! The idea of seeing each day that you have achieved your target (in this instance the number of days you've not drank) can make it seem like a lot more achievable. This can be achieved by hanging a calendar and marking every day with markers or a red pen to demonstrate that you have achieved your goal . You can also use markers or a black pen to mark off days that weren't able to complete.

Patience is the key. Humans are built to seek things faster and will satisfy us fast. We rarely think about or consider the longer-term benefits as often. This means be patient with yourself and remembering the fact that regardless of whether you screw out, you'll are able to heal and feel appreciated for your efforts.

Remove any distractions from your objective. In this instance, you should get the alcohol out of your home. If you live with your roommates, request that they take the drinks in their rooms, with an additional trash bin where they can dispose of the cans and bottles when they're done, or something similar to that. It's easy to fall for when you are seeing it all the day.

Make it more difficult! It's likely that you're trying to stop drinking. How much more can they go? Let your family and friends know about what's going on and say, "If I mess up and drink, I'll have to take this action instead. Be sure to follow through the process." A lot of important people around you are more than willing to assist (either to help you or simply because they think it will make them laugh). You can promise to give money, or do 100 push-ups in one sitting, or do anything else!

Move around. Walking around, working out or running, using the stairs instead of the elevator and so on. are all great ways to exercise. It is possible to boost your energy levels to stay on top of your goal , or to cause you to be tired enough that you won't get distracted. In this scenario, feeling tired is beneficial. However, it might not be beneficial when your objective is like finishing your work in the shortest time possible!

These are the most effective methods I have come across or consider as efficient ways to get yourself back up and gain drive to be in the top position to achieve your goals!

What do you think about patience? What can you do to be patient? Let's look at it!

Be patient and remain positive

Again, this is among the most vital, but also extremely difficult tasks to complete.

The most important factors to remind you to remain patient include:

It's important to remember that you're human Things can only happen so fast

Remember that everyone makes mistakes, and you will be back to the same place you were after making a mistake

Inability to meet your daily goals does not mean you're a success; if you keep striving, you're making progress!

Every thing takes time to realize their full potential, which includes getting to your destination

Everybody is different. Just that you believe someone is doing more than you, it doesn't necessarily mean you're more valuable than they are, it's simply that you're at a different speed.

These are most likely the best ways to get started. However, it can be difficult to manage, particularly in the case of a bad health condition. Motivation and optimism can be too exhausting to sustain at times.

Then, come back to the support group. They'll likely tell you similar stories or suggest you join in on something fun together to improve your mood. Sometimes, just knowing that someone is concerned and truly believes that you're doing a great job is the only thing you require to feel good about the things you're doing.

Positivity can be hard to nurture often. Liminal thinking could be a factor here as well to aid you. However, sometimes having a moment to yourself can help you get more done. Relax and eat a delicious meal or watch a movie you've always wanted to see, or go through your favorite TV shows. The ability to relax your brain by engaging in a task that doesn't require a lot of effort from your mind is sometimes the best method to get back from feeling depressed.

Discuss your feelings or record them in a journal. Sometimes, you need to let the feelings out of your system in some way. It's better to speak to someone, write it down or get it out of your system rather than getting angry over your loved ones.

Chapter 15: The Steps to Get Rid of Alcohol

You can beat your addiction to alcohol. There will be times you feel that you are unable to control your cravings. However, you must remember that you're a lot more powerful than the desire to drink. These are steps to follow to stop drinking:

You can empower yourself, not your addiction to alcohol.

If you are feeling weak in the face of your addiction, you have keep in mind that drinking has no power against you. Don't let your self or other people to convince you contrary. When you begin to believe that you're not invincible against alcoholism, then you'll be able to start the fight to beat it. You are in control of your body and can decide what you would like to consume and what you do not want to.

Find your weaknesses.

Through the years you may have discovered the distinct kinds of alcohol that you are most fond of. It is likely that you enjoy alcohol more than hard drinks or in reverse. Making the most of your personal experiences can assist you in tackling the issue that is making it difficult to quit drinking.

For instance, if you observe that on working hours, you consume several beers a day with your coworkers after work, and on weekdays when your closest friends invite you to go out for a drink or two more, then you are aware of the places you should be working on stopping your drinking habits. Start exploring other options to pass your time other than drinking with colleagues at work or with your pals. You could take up something new that you are able to concentrate on in order to stay away from going out for drinks. On weekends, you can begin planning hikes or other activities to keep free of drinking.

It is crucial to conduct an assessment of the when the reason, and why of your drinking habits to identify your weaknesses. This is an all-in-one major one in overcoming the alcoholism.

Find the compelling reasons you have to quit.

There are many compelling reasons that could motivate you to cut down on alcohol consumption including your mental and spiritual health to your relationships with family and friends to your work and of course you physical well-being. Write your reasons for why you are so convinced and go through the list at least two times per throughout the day (one early in the day, and the other in the evening). It is a good idea to keep adding more reasons to your list to stay engaged and motivated. You'll find it more easy to conquer your addiction to alcohol with more convincing reasons to take action.

It is essential to recognize that other people's reasons for quitting do not necessarily need to be the reasons you choose to quit. In this process it is essential to discover the true motives that are important to you. This is an individual task and you don't need to discuss it with anyone other than yourself. Don't hesitate to share reasons that are personal or private to you. Be sure to include reasons even if consider them embarrassing. It's easy to record your reasons in a spot that you only have access to. It is best to keep an item that is handy to check your list anytime you're tempted to drink.

Imagine your healthful self.

If you're feeling down or unhappy One of the most effective ways to help yourself feel more positive is to visualize yourself as your "clean self" and the kind healthy, satisfying, and abundant life waiting to you in the coming years. Be aware that your life's future begins at the moment you decide to be free from alcohol addiction. The moment that you decide to stop drinking is when you start to get healthier. Your future isn't defined by the past actions you took. It's defined by the choices you make to take now. Don't be a slave to your bad choices you've made in the past , so you can focus on the actions you're going to do today to make this a better day.

Everyday you should take a moment to visualize your happier and healthier self. Concentrate on this person, not the person you were. If you decide to do this each day and you'll soon be amazed to find your dream person imagined has come to life.

Choose which company you will maintain.

If you have close family members who's lives revolve around alcohol, it is important be careful to not be around those who drink. You can inform them that you're open to spending time with them and engage in activities that aren't related to drinking. If they aren't averse to this, then you're better off finding new acquaintances who will help you through your journey to recovery. You will always find ways to be more comfortable in being with other people. Making an effort to remain in positive surroundings and be in a healthy environment will pay off in the end. It will be clear how satisfying your life could be when you're successful in achieving your objectives because you're not ruled by your addiction.

Change your lifestyle.

The man who said it is Albert Einstein who said that insaneness is the act of doing the same thing repeatedly, expecting different outcomes. It is only possible to fully overcome your addiction by changing your approach to things. That means you have to make many adjustments in your home as well as within your daily routine, generally. The first and most important thing is that you should throw out any alcohol you're keeping at home or at work. This will keep your from being enticed to drink more. If you have to be able take an alternative route from workplace to home (or reverse the process) to avoid going to the bar in the area in which you typically drink. Also, you should begin thinking about new and healthier things that you can engage in while you consume alcohol. If you've resisted eating healthy meals due to your drinking habits, you'll should begin to learn new ways to consume healthy food throughout the day. This will assist your body recuperate faster from the effects of alcohol.

It is important to reiterate this once more: you have the ability to create the life you desire for your family and yourself. If you are committed to perseverance, determination and persistence to make the necessary changes, you'll eventually be able to do things differently and everything you do will improve.

Chapter 16: Negative Side Effects of Drinking underage

The reasons for underage drinking

There isn't a single reason to drink under the age of 18 In this section, we will look at the most frequent motives.

A typical reason for young people to start drinking is the fact that the adults in their lives are using different substances. If they witness people who smoke, drink or consume other substances and they are exposed to the same things increase. Additionally, young people enjoy the idea of trying new things. Another reason is because they watch the people they know smoke or drink. When they are urged by their peers to have a drink, odds of them agreeing to such requests are very high. Although it may sound cliche teens believe the drinking of alcohol to be aspect of a teenager's life.

When the media begin to popularize drinks culture the young are enticed to believe it's acceptable to drink. If they watch the actors, singers or other characters in a TV show smoke or drink and think that they ought to try this. If young adults are feeling unsatisfied or cannot find a way to release all of their emotions They may resort to alcohol. Dependent on the kind of substance they choose to use, they could be able to feel joy or energy and confidence. The teenage years are not simple, and the process of growing older itself can have a negative impact on the wellbeing of a teenager. There are numerous instances where teens begin using prescription drugs to manage the stress in their life or for managing it. Sometimes, they use prescription stimulants to give them extra energy needed to boost their ability to concentrate and concentrate. In addition, they begin using alcohol since it allows them to escape from their sour life.

Alcohol is a great way to get rid of any inhibitions. If a teenager is shy and shy, it is possible that he believes that drinking alcohol can make him feel more confident. Alcohol can alter the way that the person perceives reality and makes choices. If a small amount of this rationality goes out of the way, it becomes much more easy to let go of any repressed urges.

Another reason that is often cited for uninitiated alcohol consumption is boredom. A mind that is empty is the perfect place for the devil. Teenagers who are afraid of being in a room by themselves have difficulty finding something to do or looking for thrills. The most likely source of this kind of excitement is alcohol. In addition, alcohol provides the opportunity to connect with others who are like-minded and also provides them with an opportunity to socialize.

Instant gratification is a tempting proposition to everyone and not only teens. But, the ability of teenagers to consciously examine the consequences of their decisions is lower than that of adults. Therefore, their minds are developing. frequently succumb to the desire for immediate gratification. Alcohol is an excellent source of instant satisfaction that teenagers seek. They do not just know the effects alcohol has on them, but also how they can quickly achieve the desired outcomes. For example, if a teenager believes that he'll feel better after having a few drinks, his primary motive to drink is to be more relaxed.

The teens and the era of rebellion run hand-in-hand. In adolescence, the children struggle to overcome their childhood ways and forming an adult, mature persona. In this transitional period children engage in diverse acts of rebellion in order to establish their limits. Alcohol is their preferred method of rebellion.

Harmful consequences of underage drinking

The body of a young person is still developing, and drinking alcohol that is not supervised could seriously hinder this growth. Drinking alcohol at a young age also puts people more susceptible to long-term mental and physical damage that is caused by alcohol use.

Drinking underage, particularly regular and frequent drinking can lead to a range of negative effects. The adverse effects of drinking alcohol could be a quick and acute consequence of a single instance of alcohol consumption that has led to impairment in functioning. This can lead to tragic injuries or even accidental deaths. The consequences of drinking alcohol may be cumulative and numerous, leading to low school performance as well as broken relationships and addiction. According to research, it's thought that around 70% of those who drink excessively are at greater chance of making bad decisions that have long-term consequences when they reach the age of 19 or 20. But, those who are underage don't necessarily need to drink heavily to be at risk of negative consequences. The risk of accidents that result from driving under the influence of alcohol is more prevalent in adolescents than adults, according to a few studies. Also teenagers and young adults do not necessarily need to drink heavily in order to increase the risk of suffering adverse consequences.

Research has also shown that people who engage in drinking underage are at a higher risk of suffering from various health issues like headaches, insomnia and weight gain that is unhealthy.

Most people don't consider the first time they have had alcohol very seriously. It's not surprising that around three out of every 10 teens who consume alcohol suffer from negative consequences due to their drinking. In this article we will look at the various risks that come with drinking underage.

Alcohol Poisoning

Drinking excessively in a short time can lead to alcohol poisoning. When you are suffering from alcohol poisoning, the concentration of alcohol is too high that it causes negative consequences on the various areas of the brain that control speech and balance. Also, it damages the nerves that control the heartbeat and breathing. Also, it drastically decreases body temperature, which can lead to hypothermia. Alcohol poisoning may also affect gag reflexes, which increases the chance of death by choking and especially when vomiting. More than 4,000 hospitalizations due to underage drinking due to poisoning by alcohol were reported in the year 2014.

Injury

Drinking alcohol does not just affect the physical and mental capabilities of your body However, it also affects your judgement and coordination. This is true not just for adults however, but also in adolescents users. All of these elements can lead to accidents and may even cause injuries. Your body's weight and capacity to process alcohol determine your level of intoxication. Because the body's weight and metabolism of alcohol are very lower in younger adults this leads to an acute and rapid intoxication. Certain studies suggest that students who tested positive for alcohol had a higher danger of becoming injured or causing accidents compared to those who did not drink.

Acute Impairment

Alcohol affects the ability of people to make informed choices. As a result, minor drinkers are more at likelihood of engaging in risky behavior that could result in injuries and illness or, even death. The severe consequences of excessive and frequent drinking could cause injuries that are not intentional and even death when the driving process or dangerous behavior after drinking. The most frequent risky behavior after drinking are the following: violence, homicides as well as suicide attempts, sexual assault and sexually risky behavior and vandalism. In a number of research investigations, researchers found that those who began drinking prior to the age of 15 were twelve times more likely suffer accidental injuries while intoxicated by alcohol as compared to those who wait until age 21 before starting drinking. These same studies also revealed that those who drink underage are seven 10-fold more likely get involved in car crash or physical fight, respectively after having drank.

Driving while impaired

Driving while under the influence of alcohol have attracted a lot of attention from the media and focused policymaking in recent times. A number of laws have been enacted to limit the permissible blood alcohol level (BAC) concentrations for minor drivers to nearly zero or 0.02 at the very most. There's been a significant decrease in the number of motor vehicles driven by underage drivers that have been killed due to drinking, but it's still a significant amount. Based on the information gathered by the National Highway Traffic Safety Administration It is estimated that 69% of teenagers who died in accidents involved drinking underage in the 2,000. Drinking and driving of alcohol is not just a problem for drivers under the age of 18 as well as for the innocent victims. While only 7% licensed drivers in 2000 were aged between the ages 15 and 20 years old, they comprised 13% of drivers who died in motor vehicle crashes by drunken driving.

Thus, it's possible to conclude that the odds of minor drivers being involved in accidents are very high when they're drinking in comparison to drivers who didn't drink while driving. It's not only about driving while when drunk, but the decisions they make that are associated with their safety can be diminished when they are drunk. For instance, in the findings of a study, it is found that younger people tend to not buckle the seat belt when in a vehicle and have a higher likelihood to be into a vehicle even when the driver is drunk. Unfortunately, 40% of regular heavy drinkers confessed that they were in vehicles with a drunk driver.

Brain Development

The brain is developing during the teenage and childhood years. Drinking excessively negatively impacts memory, ability to respond, learn and remain focused. These factors are all extremely crucial during school. Therefore, excess alcohol consumption during this time can be detrimental to your education. Research indicates that kids who drink alcohol prior to 13 years old are at greater chance of having poor scores, dropping out of school, or being kicked out of school.

The excessive and continuous consumption of alcohol can harm the physical development of the brain's structure, as per new research. The brain's growth through childhood and infanthood mainly is focused on the creation of new brain cells that have numerous connections different brain cells in the way is possible. As we enter the teenage years the focus shifts to producing many neurons to creating efficient and efficient neural pathways. There are two methods by which the creation process occurs.

The first method is that the neuron's structure is altered due to the myelin sheath that surrounds it. Myelin sheath aids in the faster flow of electrical impulses in the brain. It basically implies that the capacity for an adult brain to transmit information from one area within the brain the next is quite superior to children. In adolescence, this function is located in the prefrontal as well as frontal lobes. These are the two areas of the brain that are responsible for many important aspects like organization, planning, as well as the ability to stop an impulse.

The other change that occurs with the growth of the brain is due with synaptic refinement. Synaptic refinement refers to the procedure by which the brain cells gets fine-tuned to ensure that only the pathways that are efficient remain, and the inefficient ones are cut off. Similar to the development of the sheath myelin this process can increase the speed and effectiveness of relaying and transmitting information from one region within the brain the next. This, in turn increases your reaction time overall. As you enter your teens the brain begins to undergo various changes that take place in the regions of the brain that are responsible for critically evaluating the effects of your actions as well as the capacity to effectively manage stress.

In a study on animals it was discovered that alcohol consumption in adolescents can cause harm to the brain's processes and development. The study involved rats who were exposed to high and frequent doses of alcohol in order to replicate the drinking habits of an adolescent who is a heavy drinker.

Mental Health

One of the main reasons for underage drinking is because young people turn to alcohol to cope. They believe that alcohol can keep them sane and helps to ease anxiety about their issues. Also, excessive drinking of alcohol over a prolonged period may cause a number of mental health issues. There is evidence suggesting that there is a connection between mental health issues and the use of alcohol.

Substance Use and Abuse

Drinking too much in a young adult can be a problem by itself however, it can also be directly linked to other dangerous actions, like the consumption of illegal substances. In comparison to those who do not drink there is a higher chance of users of cannabis, tobacco or other hard-drugs are excessive, according to certain research.

Accidental injuries

Alcohol does not only cause an impairment in judgement and poor decision-making, it also affects the body's coordination. This is among the main reasons that alcohol is the most significant reason for injuries that occur unintentionally. The majority of accidental accidents and deaths caused by reckless and dangerous behavior in addition to driving is due to alcohol consumption. In a study that was conducted during 1999, researchers discovered that 40% of the victims of underage and injuries, including drowning, burns, and falls, were all positive for high concentrations of alcohol. It's not just accidental injuries from traffic accidents however, alcohol can be involved in deaths and injuries caused by suicidal behavior and violence, too. Alcohol consumption that is excessive and frequent can cause the development of negative emotions like despair depression, suicidal thoughts and suicide attempts.

According to statistics published from the Centers for Disease Control and Prevention in 2001, it was found in 2001 that alcohol consumption was the main factor in 36% of murders as well as in 8% and 12% of male and female suicides respectively, among those under the 21 years of age. In a study published by 1994's National Centre on Addiction and

Substance Abuse and the National Centre on Addiction and Substance Abuse, it was discovered that around 95% of violent crimes and 95 percent of the rapes perpetrated by college students on campuses of colleges involved alcohol consumption by the perpetrator, the victim or both.

Sexual Activity

Another problems with alcohol is sexual violence, sexually unplanned and even unprotected sexual activities. In a book entitled "A A Call for Action Redefining the culture of drinking in U.S. Colleges," it was revealed that more than 70 thousand students in the ages between 18 and 24 were the victims of alcohol-related date sexual assault or rape. A few studies have also suggested an increase in sexual assault and date rapes on college campuses reveal drinking alcohol to be one of causes hindering the behavior of the attackers and victims.

It's not just the risk of being a victim sexual assault or being the victim of it; teens who drink more often are more at likelihood of engaging in sexually risky actions and behaviors. According to an investigation which was conducted, approximately 44 percent of teenagers who were sexually active said they were most likely to have sexual relations when they drink. Alcohol can cause impairment in judgment and, consequently, the odds of making decision that is rational when you are drinking are very small. Therefore, someone who would be averse to engaging in sexually risky behaviors is more likely engage in sexual behavior being under influence.

Alcohol also decreases inhibitions and is among the main factors that lead to dangerous behaviors. Young people are more likely to drink even if they are aware that alcohol affects their decision-making abilities and causes people to indulge in sexual activity that they wouldn't normally engage in have if they were in a clean state. In a survey of college students that was conducted by Boston University School of Public Health it was discovered that people who had their first drink prior to the time they reached the age of 13 are twice as likely to indulge in unplanned sexual activity and are twice as likely to engage sexual activity that is not secured.

Property Deterioration

A different set of consequences that are associated with activities and behavior that are influenced by alcohol includes vandalism and damage to property. According to a study there is a belief that the probability of drunk teenagers engaging in these actions regardless of their age, are quite high, particularly on campuses of colleges, they are compared with sober students.

Long-Term Impacts

The long-term consequences of a single choice made while under drinking alcohol are evident. One of the immediate repercussions could be the death of a person or injury, however each of these outcomes have long-term consequences as well. In addition, drinking excessively alcohol in the early years can have long-term effects on youth's chances in the future. Anyone who begins drinking alcohol before 15 are at greater risk of battling long-term issues. For instance, those who drink before age 15 have a higher chance of developing an alcohol dependency later in life. Furthermore, the likelihood of developing dependence on alcohol in the near future is around 40% among these young people and just 10% for those who begin drinking after they have reached the legal drinking age according to the findings of a study.

Frequent and excessive consumption of alcohol is often connected to depression in the form of low self-esteem, social behavior, dependence on other substances and anxiety. In a study the authors found that about 25% of students who performed poorly in college were regular drinkers. Drinkers who are underage are, consequently more at risk of developing any of the health issues mentioned in the earlier chapter.

Chapter 17: Actions to Recovery and Avoiding Relapses

Being sober is an important stage in the process of stopping drinking however it's only the start of your lengthy journey. While doctors and rehabilitation centers can assist you during the initial phases to quit, they do not offer the long-term advantages you want to enjoy for so long as you don't make any adjustments to your life. It is important to remember that the greatest change needs to be yours and should be in the context of your life style and how you view things regarding your daily life. It is also about how you face the temptation that is presented before you. Here are some actions you can adopt to lead a sober way of life:

Maintain a healthy lifestyle. It is a great way to stay clear of shifts in your mindset and also avoid desires for alcohol is to learn to appreciate yourself. Make sure you are having a healthy and balanced lifestyle by getting plenty of sleeping every night, eating a balanced diet and working out every day. Exercise can help your body release endorphins, which aid in reducing stress and maintaining a healthy well-being.

Make sure you surround yourself with people who can support you. It is crucial to have as much support you can. Connect with people who could positively influence you and those who will help you feel confident about yourself. Spending time with these people will force you to realize how much you'll lose if you return to drinking. This will keep you focused on quitting.

Find new interests and activities. Your schedule should be filled with activities that will keep you away from drinking. You can either take part in a volunteer activity or find some new sports to enjoy with your pals.

Join support groups. Support groups are an excellent method to maintain your journey. The people who oversee support groups have been through similar experiences stopping drinking and their experience can help you understand the benefits of to stop drinking.

You can change your approach to dealing with stress. Most of the time, the reason you turn to alcohol when you're having a problem is that you do not know how to manage these issues on your own. Find ways to cope with stressand anxiety, and make sure it's beneficial and healthy that includes engaging in exercises, breathing exercises meditation, or other methods to relax.

Speak "no". No matter how many people are trying to get you to drink during social events, always reply by saying a polite but clear "no thank you". You can't avoid going to places where you'll be asked to drink.

Beware of the temptation. It is of course helpful by removing any items that may remind that you drink when you make the decision to stop. Eliminate any alcohol you might have at home, or look for ways that your drinking buddies are willing to do.

Chapter 18: Disappearing Time Trick

The dark magician definitely has some amazing tricks up his sleeves. Perhaps one of the most popular is the 'disappearing trick'. When I was an avid drinker, I would regularly request that this trick be repeated just once more. The cause was stress. this desire, and possibly nothing more likely to make me run to the store for booze than the prospect of bad news waiting in my mailbox at the conclusion of a tiring day at work. Doom was handed to me earlier in the morning by the mailman. I would drink to deal with the annoyances of life. I got so accustomed to living in a semi-alcoholic sleep that life was becoming increasingly difficult, something I would try to get out of.

When I got back from work and saw the credit card bill lying on the floor, waiting for my attention, and eventually it caught the eyes of my used check book , I would swiftly put the envelope in an assortment of junk mail before heading right to the local liquor shop. Whiskey was my weapon of choice for destroying the thoughts that were lingering in my mind and shut off my excessive imagination. If the credit card's banana skin was only a few times every month, that might be acceptable. However, at the height of my drinking, I was spending $5000 per year on alcohol. That is one of the main reasons there were seven credit card accounts all growing in the midst of my increasing debt. The easily identifiable envelopes from the companies that issued them were often found on my doorstep and made my home time an emotional risk. I claimed that I'd worked hard at work and could enjoy an evening at home during the evening when I was not spent worrying about the expenses. Of course, my definition of "quality time" was sitting in a state that was near conscious watching the TV before falling asleep approximately 8 pm. My bedtime was earlier than many toddlers and infants!

It is only now that I realize that whether the bill was paid or not, it didn't matter. I did not stop drinking but maybe because of a different motive. The most convincing argument I had to myself was that I wasn't an alcohol addict but instead an over-thinker of traditional size. I could not keep my thoughts from ruminating over any minor issue and then exaggerating the issue to the point of causing a catastrophe. I used alcohol to stop my thoughts and to shift the issue ahead to one day. I was able to do this for real problems which actually existed, but as well with many imagined issues that I was equally likely to think of. Today , I am able to tell people that I've experienced some terrible things in my life, yet only 20 percent of them actually took place.

Naturally, I should have seen the warning signal earlier. it's okay to chat with yourself, but when you start to respond then you'll know you're in trouble. We who are problem drinkers get proficient at not seeing the obvious signs of bleeding, in favor of a highly precariously placed reason to continue to be in love with the substance we love to.

As a youngster being raised within the North East of England my granddad Jack used to play the same 'magic coins from the ear' trick each whenever he saw me. As a young child who loved his grandpa it wasn't long before me to realize that I was not in my peripheral view that his coin was present in his hands at the time it was taken out of his pocket. I would often challenge him about the truthfulness of the trick and he would then rant in a hilarious and exaggerated defense while pretending to be upset at the suggestion that a magician as skilled like him could cheat. The trick always made me smile, and I was amazed at the joy my granddad felt from performing the trick for me. I'd pay any amount to have him here every day to perform the trick again for me. Alcohol is a fan of a similarly awkward illusion known as the Disappearing time trick'. It does it often since we are unable to notice the ungainly slight of hand which makes it about as far as it gets.

The desire to avoid the world is among the most frequently cited motives I hear for explaining the need to drink alcohol. The problem with alcohol to avoid life is that it allows the user to move through time and to consciously erase all worries and stressors that are pressuring (as they believe it can). Alcohol consumption is actually a pausing button on the CD player at the dawn, and once the anaesthetic wears off, the track starts playing at the exact point it was in the night prior to. There is not a single second of misery was missed; it's been preserved and stored to play at a later time. The infamous 'Disappearing Time trick turns out to be nothing more than just illusions and smoke. The dark magician who created it drinking aficionado, the drinker has the complication of the problems from yesterday to contend with in addition to the issues that are certain to come up today.

This alcohol-related function reminds me of a funny (and sometimes painfully sad) film starring Adam Sandler called 'Click'. A feisty architect named Michael Newman, played by Sandler is able to make a deal with the Devil and is granted an universal remote control that can do the normal things you'd expect from an item, like turning on the TV or opening the garage doors , but it also has the ability to effortlessly control life itself. Michael soon realizes how he can delight in the fact that at the press of a button, he is able to speed up the pace of time or even skip certain events altogether. Michael stumbles upon this incredible feature of the remote while in frigid temperatures, waiting for his pet to get a drink before going to bed. The dog is smitten playing in the yard and is oblivious to the urging to "do his work" being sounded by his angry and cold owner. In a bizarre way, Newman is pointing the remote at the dog and presses on the speed forward feature. In a blur of action including the rather offensive arm cocking Newman is awestruck by the potential of his new gadget.

As the story progresses, he utilizes the remote in increasing amounts and avoids fights with his wife moving forward boring visits from his parents and then, erroneously believing his soon to be promoted to a higher position at work, he requests the remote to skip to the day when he becomes a the team of architects. He doesn't realize that the fact that his promotion was more than a decade away. the remote is an intelligent gadget which learns about the habits of its user and attempts to predict the future. It assumes that since it has stayed away from such events as sexual relations in with wife spending time with his children christmas and birthday parties and that in the future, they will not wish to attend these events. Then, it turns off his objections and instantly forward through the most precious and memorable moments in our lives. At the final scene of the film we meet an old obese, sick and obese Michael Newman who is distraught due to the fact that he's missed his kids growing older and lost his wife to a different man, and has sold his soul in order to become the most profitable partner in the business. He is utterly depressed and is resentful over the loss of every moment that make life worth living.

I've watched the film more than a dozen times. I may have even watched it several times with an enormous glass of whiskey on my hands. It's absolutely obvious as to how the universal remote in the same film plays exactly the same function as alcohol.

Alcohol is a bargain with people, but much like a scammed insurance salesperson, it fails to inform them of the tiny print. The promise is to help make the issues disappear, and while it may keep its word, but what it fails to mention until it's past the point of no return is that issue are likely to recur the following day but bigger than they were before. Like a gambling addict, who is chasing his losses seeking a huge payoff, now the problems are getting exponentially larger and more difficult to deal with. In a state of panic, unable to handle the flood of anxiety, the gambler must create a new, more significant arrangement with devil. the seemingly impossible cycle starts to take shape.

Natasha's Story

Natasha Foreman was the life and spirit at the office. She was not only the top sales executive for nearly a decade, always hitting target after target, but she was also the one to bring all the employees together. In times of good times, she organized the parties and when the team was struggling she urged unification and the spirit of the team. The thing that was not noticed by everyone initially was that the seeming positive aspects of her leadership created chances to drink. If the sales team exceeded their monthly goals, Natasha would declare that 'on Friday night, we're going out for a celebration'. She came up with a concept called "Pink Payday's," which was a simple way of saying that a crate full of champagne pink was given to the team on the final Friday of the month, when they were paid. The idea was pitched to her bosses and persuaded that they would pay for it , arguing that it would create a positive environment and encourage positive morale.

If Natasha was the only one who drank during those events, the reasons she had for arranging such incentives for the team would be laudable. Actually, Natasha was beginning to create her schedule solely around drinking opportunities. If a large-spending client was scheduled to renew an agreement, it was simple for her to justify an expensive lunch in her expenses form. Despite the growing problems, she was as reliable and as successful as ever throughout her career.

She was awed by the freedom that her colleagues gave her, and the work was fun, but like all nine-to-fiveers, she was wishing for the week in order to make it to the weekend. On Friday nights, Natasha would talk about that she was anticipating spending a few days of relaxing time with her family and husband. When she was in the sales meeting on Monday morning, meeting, she would listen to the many stories of amazing experiences and family outings colleagues of hers had enjoyed during the preceding few days . She would then look at her head in awe.

"I am not sure how you guys manage to find enough time for all this. We had a grocery shop and then what about one thing, and the other was the weekend completed. They move too fast, don't you think" She would often declare.

The truth is that, just like the use of medical anesthetics, alcohol takes time. It doesn't matter if have surgery scheduled to undergo a triple bypass that lasts about six hours or the removal of a toenail that is ingrown which takes just six minutes, your view of the time it takes will be similar. From your perspective the moment you begin counting down to ten and in a matter of seconds, the nurse will explain that you're in the recovery area and the procedure was successful.

Natasha would begin the weekend with a Saturday breakfast full of positive thoughts and promises of all the activities they would be doing as a unit as an entire family. Jenny as well as Brad who were nine and 7 bounced over the walls with joy as they listened to mom discuss possibilities of visiting the zoo or traveling upstate to amusement parks. The fun things that they enjoyed were not always available since the weekly shopping at the supermarket was the first thing to do and all plans could be altered in the same aisle of the supermarket.

At the end of the aisle Natasha had decided that tomorrow was the ideal time to go on the trip. She had compelling reasons to justify her delay, when she wandered between spirits, wine before moving on to beer. "The traffic is going to be terrible today", she mused aloud "besides it's already 11am, and half of the day is gone'. To ease the guilt over letting her kids let them down (again) the mother would explain to them that the trip was postponed , and try to redress the hurt and tears by sticking them with the latest toy or Disney DVD. She would try to sell these (just the same way she would market advertising at work) with the concept that it was Movie Afternoon... everyone sitting in front of the TV with chips, popcorn and dips. Doesn't that sound like fun?

The kids were easily distracted, however there were hints of disappointment. The movie was always less entertaining than what it was portrayed in the commercial. Sure, Buzz and Woody could not help but entertain and indeed, there was chips and popcorn just as promised, however mom who was lying in her couch with a bottle of wine by her feet didn't really feel like she was part of the fun. in. The children would be laughing over the fun slap stick caps on the screen, and then turn to tell their mom about their favorite character only to realize that her eyes were shut and she missed the most enjoyable part of the film.

Natasha would awake in the dark, with the television was now asleep on 'stand by', and the home quiet. Jenny and Brad were long ago put to bed by Their Dad and he was off to bed on his own as was the norm. A mixture of regret and hangovers was rushing through her awake mind, and as she walked down the stairs, she would promise herself that tomorrow was going to be a better one. Sunday is about spending time with the family and spending time with them. The woman would pretend to lie while she struggled to get dressed and lie down alongside her husband, who was sleeping.

Sunday's intentions were changed by an event that led to an increase in alcohol consumption. Before Natasha was aware of what had happened, she was in the sales meeting on Monday asking how the other salespeople were able to accomplish so much in just a short amount of time.

We ask for alcohol to perform some magic for us. We beg it to make our troubles disappear, and often it seems to have accomplished exactly this. In reality, David Copperfield never really made the Statue of Liberty disappear, and alcohol did not solve our troubles in the least for a second. Astonishingly, as we watched the magician's act we didn't see the pickpocket in action. In the distance, the hand reached into our pockets and looked through the contents. There was cash, and some valuable trinkets in the pocket, but the criminal stole the most valuable thing we own... our time. It doesn't matter how much you put in or how much you bargain or how lucky you are the only thing you cannot get more of is your time.

Chapter 19: Remain Sober and Take Advantage Of The Rewards

If you've been successful in your endeavor to stop drinking the habit of drinking, you'll have to maintain this habit throughout your life in order to reap the amazing benefits it brings. If you're thinking "how do I maintain my pace?", then don't be concerned. It's not too difficult once you are familiar with this new routine. You'll be pleasantly surprised by your ability to continue to improve and devising strategies to aid you in keeping your vow. Alcohol will no longer be an object of attraction when you notice how much more relaxed you are and how much your family members appreciate you and how wonderful life can be. You are able to do anything and be a vital part of your circle of friends without drinking. It's just a matter of learning to be able to say "no" in the face of alcohol, without being rude, or giving in to the temptation. Your life will be lived in its fullest once you have stopped drinking.

For some who are struggling to keep going with this new direction. This is due to the fact that they have achieved their short-term goals but don't prepare for the long term. You are prepared to face this "big change" by going through various ways to reach your goal. That's great! But what if you decide to stay the same way for the rest of your life? What happens if the cravings don't diminish and you want to drink? What happens if you fall into a relapse? These are the main questions to be asking yourself after going through that phase where you determinedly tried to quit alcohol. Don't give up! You are more powerful than what you think. Here are few guidelines that can assist you in keeping sober:

Dispose of Alcohol

The first step is to dispose of alcohol once you have achieved your objective. Locate all the containers and bottles, then empty them into the sink, then dump them into the garbage. Do not store a single bottle in your home, keeping the guests' needs in your mind. It's perfectly fine for you to offer your guests coffee, tea or soft drinks, as well as lemonade. This can useful when you're tempted to drink.

Anti-Denial Policy and Accepting Responsibility

People who have an alcohol addiction lie to themselves by refusing to admit the fact that they've done something wrong. They blame the shoulders of others or another factor to conceal the root of their problem drinking and their behavior. They do not accept accountability for their mistakes. The situation will never improve when you follow this pattern. Therefore, it's best to implement a denial-free policy and accept responsibility for what you do. If you fall back then accept it and begin your fight over again. This way, you don't have be lying to your self or to anyone else. Once you've stopped denying the facts, you'll notice the difference.

Say No to Alcohol

It is now the moment to say no any drinks being offered by your friends , or in social gatherings. A simple word "no" can keep you from returning to the old ways of drinking. You're trying to quit drinking completely, therefore you must take good care of yourself. If you're not willing to share your story with certain individuals, like your relatives, friends and colleagues , or even your university or college colleagues, you could simply create reasons you are comfortable with. It is possible to say that alcohol is causing you terrible headaches and it causes stomach upset or makes you feel exhausted, or you're taking antibiotics or supplements. Simply saying "No thank you" as well as any reason can help you.

Be flexible and believe in yourself.

If you've tried a few methods to reduce your cravings, but they did not work then don't be a victim. Try to look at these instances in a positive manner. It is important to think that to yourself "It did not work due to this cause. I'll do the same thing in a different manner this opportunity." Should you have gave into your inclination, don't fret that it's no big deal. It is important to learn from every mistake you make and attempt to do things in a more efficient method. Don't stop, continue to work hard and you'll be successful in the end. Find success stories to inspire you This will be a great aid you.

Second, confront your challenges and the world without the aid of alcohol. If you drink to forget about your issues, you're lying to yourself and burying you feet in the sand as an Ostrich. This won't make your issues go away or ease the depression. This will only make the situation worse. Remind yourself that you're not an addict, and that your a mature man capable of handling everything. Remember why you quit drinking initially and you'll be able take on any situation, alcohol-free.

You can keep yourself busy

The best method to ensure that alcohol is not on your head is to keep active. If you're an undergraduate, you should be engaged in school or sports, as well as other extracurricular activities. If you're a housewife or mom, be vigilant for your children. You should be occupied with household chores and shopping, fitness classes or any other activity that you are interested in. If you are employed it's great. You'll be able to spend time with your family or with friends at home after work. Plan your weekend activities Fix anything that requires repair cook and exercise or write, paint or do whatever you want to do (that does not involve drinking)! This is the most effective way to stay occupied during times when you're tempted to drink.

Conclusion

I hope the information contained in this book was beneficial to you. That's my pleasure! "Self Aid guide to Overcoming Alcoholism" It is a guidebook that was created to meet your needs. The book has been written in a step-by step order following thorough and thorough research with individuals with similar experiences as well as health professionals.

"Self Help Guide for Beating Alcoholism" is all you need to lead a happy life. I'm sure you're currently sober, or you've planned how to quit drinking and begin a new life. Follow the steps described in the book's breakthrough. this book. You might not have to be to follow all of them, however you must modify your approach and only apply the ones that are suitable for your needs. Also, taking into consideration of seeking medical attention provides you with an added and amazing benefit.

It is the next stage to start the recovery program and establish an active life. If you find this book beneficial and enjoyable take the time to leave a comment. This will help others with similar issues. Your comments will be appreciated. Thank you!

www.ingramcontent.com/pod-product-compliance
Lightning Source LLC
Chambersburg PA
CBHW071835080526
44589CB00012B/1008